CONTENTS

PART ONE: INJURY PREVENTION

PART TWO: EMERGENCY REFERENCE

John Metzger

American
Red Cross

Health and Safety
Services

SPORT
SAFETY
TRAINING

INJURY PREVENTION AND CARE
HANDBOOK

StayWell

StayWell

Printed in the United States of America
Composition by Graphic World Inc.
Printing/Binding by Mail-Well Graphics

StayWell
263 Summer Street
Boston, MA 02210

Library of Congress Cataloging in Publication Data

Sport safety training : injury prevention & care handbook / the United States
   Olympic Committee & the American Red Cross.
        p.   cm.
   Includes bibliographical references.
   ISBN 0-8151-0983-0
   1. Sports—United States—Safety measures—Handbooks, manuals, etc.
2. Athletes—Health and hygiene—United States—Handbooks, manuals,
etc.   3. Sports injuries—United States—Prevention—Handbooks, manuals,
etc.   I. United States Olympic Committee. II. American Red Cross.
GV344.S67   1997
613.7'11—dc20   96-34022
                                                                    CIP

      00 01/ 9 8 7 6 5

Acknowledgments

This manual was developed through a combined effort of the American Red Cross and the United States Olympic Committee. Without the commitment to excellence of paid and volunteer staff of both organizations, this manual could not have been created.

The Health and Safety Services Sport Safety Training Development Team at American Red Cross national headquarters responsible for designing and writing this book included: Bruce M. Carney, Project Team Leader; Rhonda Starr, Project Manager; Thomas A. Bates, NREMT-B, Paul Stearns III, Associates, Educational Development; Dana N. Jessen, Manager, Program and Customer Support; Dean W. Dimke, Cathleen Reilly, Associates, Business Development and Marketing; and Jane Moore, Specialist. Administrative support was provided by Vivian Mills.

The following United States Olympic Committee staff provided guidance and review: Tom Crawford, P.E.D., Director of Coaching; Audrius Barzdukas, Associate Director of Coaching; Jan Schnittger, Manager, Coaching and Intern Programs; David Mair, Risk Manager; Sean McCann, Ph.D., Sport Psychologist; Jay T. Kearney, Ph.D., Sport Physiologist; Bob Beeten, Director, Sports Medicine; and Jenny Stone, Manager, Sports Medicine Clinical Program.

The following American Red Cross national headquarters Health and Safety Services staff provided guidance and review: Susan M. Livingstone, Vice President, Health and Safety Services; Jean Wagaman, Director, Program and Customer Support; Ferris D. Kaplan, Director, Business Development and Marketing; Earl Harbert, Manager, Contract and Financial Management; S. Elizabeth

White, M.A.Ed., Manager, First Aid/CPR and Special Projects Educational Development; Karen J. Peterson, Ph.D., Senior Associate, HIV/AIDS Educational Development; Marietta Damond, Senior Associate, Program Evaluation; Martha F. Beshers, Michael Espino, Don Vardell, Associates, Educational Development; and Jennifer Deibert, Associate, Program Evaluation.

The Mosby Lifeline Editorial and Production Team included: David Dusthimer, Vice President and Publisher; Claire Merrick, Editor-in-Chief; Stacey Wildenberg, Editor; Shannon Canty, Project Supervisor; Doug Bruce, Director, Editing, Design, Manufacturing and Production; Chris Baumle, Project Manager; Kay Kramer, Director of Art and Design; Jerry Wood, Director of Manufacturing; Theresa Fuchs, Manufacturing Manager; Pat Stinecipher, Special Product Manager; and Renee Duenow, Designer.

Special thanks go to Tom Lochhaas, developmental editor and writer; Vincent Knaus, photographer; AKA Design, Inc., cover and interior designers; Rolin Graphics, illustrators; and Richard Even, video producer/director. Cover photos courtesy ALLSPORT. Figure skater © 1994 DUOMO.

Guidance and review were also provided by members of the Sport Safety Training Development Review Group:

Alex Antoniou, Ph.D.
Aquatics Coordinator
Rutgers University
New Brunswick, New Jersey

Sandra R. Badger
Department Head, Health
Education
Doherty High School
Colorado Springs, Colorado

Michelle Dusserre-Farrell
Coaching Committee Member
United States Olympic
Committee
Colorado Springs, Colorado

Barbara Fiorina
Director, Health and Safety
American Red Cross
San Diego/Imperial County
Chapter
San Diego, California

Ron Frick
Director, Safety and Health
American Red Cross in
Greater New York
New York, New York

Michael Giles, Sr.
Aquatics Director and Risk
Manager, Recreation Sports
The University of Southern
Mississippi
Hattiesburg, Mississippi

Rita Glassman
National Youth Sports Safety
Foundation
Needham, Massachusetts

Daniel Gould, Ph.D.
Department of Exercise and
Sport Science
University of North Carolina at
Greensboro
Greensboro, North Carolina
Coaching Committee Member
United States Olympic
Committee
Colorado Springs, Colorado

Angus McBryde, M.D.
Medical University of South
Carolina
Charleston, South Carolina

Jan Schnittger
Manager, Coaching and Intern
Programs
United States Olympic
Committee
Colorado Springs, Colorado

Rob Scott
American Red Cross Bay Area
San Francisco, California

*Guidance and review were also provided by members of
the Sport Safety Training Advisory Group:*

David Joyner, M.D.
Chair, Sports Medicine
Committee
United States Olympic
Committee
Colorado Springs, Colorado

Lyle Micheli, M.D.
Associate Clinical Professor of
Orthopaedic Surgery
Harvard Medical School
Boston, Massachusetts
Director, Division of Sports
Medicine
Children's Hospital
Boston, Massachusetts

Dennis Miller, M.S., P.T., A.T.C.
Purdue University
West Lafayette, Indiana

Julie Moyer Knowles, Ed.D., A.T.C./P.T.
Health South Sports Medicine
and Rehabilitation Center
Wilmington, Delaware
Olympic Sports Medicine
Society Member

Herbert Parris, M.D.
Assistant Clinical Professor
University of Colorado Medical
School
Denver, Colorado
The Denver Center for
Sports/Family Medicine
Denver, Colorado
Olympic Sports Medicine
Society Member

External review was provided by the following chapter representatives:

Paul Krack
American Red Cross
Southwestern Indiana Chapter
Evansville, Indiana

Sandra Raborn
American Red Cross
Florida's Coast to Coast
Chapter
Daytona Beach, Florida

Ron Terwilliger
American Red Cross in Greater
New York
New York, New York

▼ How to Use This Book

The *Sport Safety Training Handbook* can be used two ways:

➤ It is an integral part of the Sport Safety Training course. It is designed to help you learn principles of injury prevention and first aid steps for specific emergency situations.

➤ It is a quick source of information for either injury prevention or emergency care. Each care section

guides your actions, step by step. Carry this book
with you, along with your first aid kit, to every
sporting event and practice.

ORGANIZATION

Sports injury research indicates that about half of all
sports injuries could be prevented.

Part One of this book, Injury Prevention, is organized
around the principles of injury prevention that apply in
many sports activities, followed by descriptions of injuries
common to many sports and specific prevention guidelines.

Part Two, Emergency Reference, is alphabetized so
that you can find needed information easily and quickly
in an emergency. For example, if someone were choking, you would find the care steps under **Choking.** Care
for eye injury is described under **Eye Injury.**

The emergency care information follows the emergency action steps described on p. viii. Always **CHECK**
the scene for safety and **CHECK** the injured or ill athlete,
CALL 9-1-1 or the local emergency number when
needed, and **CARE** for the injured or ill athlete until EMS
personnel arrive.

If you need additional information beyond the care
steps, you will be referred to related additional information. For example, when you refer to the section on **Bleeding,** that section informs you that shock is likely to occur
in someone experiencing serious bleeding and refers you
to the **Shock** section on p. 150.

In some cases, you may not know the nature of the
athlete's injury or illness. For example, if you find an athlete unconscious on the playing field but do not know the
cause, you may not know at first where to look for the
care steps. In situations like this, look under what you *do*

know. In this case, you know the athlete is unconscious, so start by looking under **Unconsciousness,** where you will be given some appropriate care steps and be directed to other potentially helpful sections.

TRAINING

Training is necessary to give you the basic information you need to prevent injury and to respond effectively in an emergency. **This book is not a substitute for training!** The American Red Cross Sport Safety Training course gives you an opportunity to learn about injury prevention, practice life-saving skills, and have questions answered by a knowledgeable instructor or referred to an appropriate resource, such as an information hotline or National Governing Body of a specific sport. Call your local American Red Cross chapter for more information on the Sport Safety Training Course.

▼ Emergency Action Steps

In any emergency, always follow the same approach to caring for the injured or ill athlete. As soon as you recognize that an emergency exists, take action.

Follow these emergency action steps:
CHECK the scene for safety; check the injured or ill athlete.
CALL 9-1-1 or the local emergency number.
CARE for the athlete.

Calling for help is often the *most important* action you can take to help the athlete in need of care.

If the athlete is unconscious, call 9-1-1 or the local emergency number immediately.

Sometimes a conscious athlete will tell you not to call EMS personnel, and you may not be sure what to do. The following will assist you in determining the appropriate response.

Always **CALL** EMS personnel if the injured athlete—

➤ Is or becomes unconscious.
➤ Is confused.
➤ Has breathing difficulty.
➤ Is not breathing or has no pulse.
➤ Has persistent chest pain or pressure.
➤ Is bleeding severely.
➤ Has pressure or pain in the abdomen that does not go away.
➤ Is vomiting or passing blood in the urine or feces.
➤ Has a seizure, severe headache, or slurred speech.
➤ Appears to have been poisoned.
➤ Has injuries to the head, neck, or back.
➤ Has possible broken bones.
➤ Has severe burns.

Also **CALL** 9-1-1 or the local emergency number for any of these situations:

➤ Fire or explosion
➤ Downed electrical wires
➤ Swiftly moving or rapidly rising water
➤ Presence of poisonous gas
➤ Vehicle collisions
➤ Athletes who cannot be moved easily

▼ First Aid Kit

Be prepared for an emergency. Keep a first aid kit nearby during all coaching and sporting activities. Whenever possible, have a second kit for multiple injury situations at a practice or competition site.

A sports first aid kit used in athletics should include the following:

➤ Adhesive bandages with gauze pads—assorted sizes
➤ Alcohol/alcohol preps
➤ Antibacterial ointment
➤ Anti-infective solution

- ➤ Antiseptic towelettes
- ➤ Arm sling (triangular bandage is fine)
- ➤ Bandage scissors
- ➤ Butterfly closures—1/8" X 3"
- ➤ Cotton swabs
- ➤ Elastic tape—2"
- ➤ Elastic wraps—2", 4", and 6"
- ➤ Emergency blanket
- ➤ Eye patch
- ➤ Eye wash
- ➤ Flashlight and batteries
- ➤ Foam padding, assorted thicknesses
- ➤ Hydrogen peroxide
- ➤ Latex/nitrile gloves (multiple pairs)
- ➤ List of emergency phone numbers
- ➤ Moleskin
- ➤ Nail clippers
- ➤ Nonstick wound dressing pads—3" X 4"
- ➤ Petroleum jelly
- ➤ Plastic bags
- ➤ Plastic bags for ice/instant ice packs
- ➤ Powder
- ➤ Resuscitation mask/face shield
- ➤ Roller gauze
- ➤ Safety pins
- ➤ Several quarters for emergency telephone calls
- ➤ *Sport Safety Training Handbook*
- ➤ Sterile gauze pads—3" X 4" or 4" X 4"
- ➤ Sunscreen
- ➤ Tape adherent
- ➤ Tape remover
- ➤ Tape underwrap
- ➤ Thermometer
- ➤ Tongue blades
- ➤ Tweezers
- ➤ White tape—1" and 1 1/2"

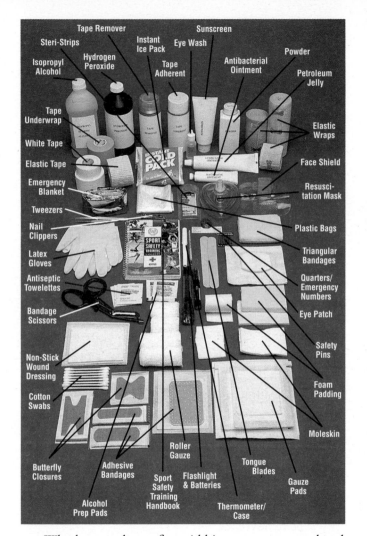

Whether you buy a first aid kit or put one together, be certain all the items previously listed are included. Check the kit regularly to make sure flashlight batteries still work and that it contains all the necessary supplies. Replace any items that have expired or been used.

INJURY PREVENTION

PART ONE

General Principles to Prevent Injury

COACHING RESPONSIBILITIES

Responsible coaching is a major factor in reducing injuries. Coaches should follow these general guidelines:

1. Remember what motivates athletes, particularly children, to play their sport. Their goal is seldom just to win or excel. Young athletes give the following as their primary reasons for being involved in athletics:
   - ➤ Have fun, enjoy excitement of competition
   - ➤ Improve skills, face challenges, learn new skills
   - ➤ Get exercise, stay in shape
   - ➤ Enjoy teamwork
2. Know the rules of the sport and insist your athletes also know and follow them. Teach your athletes to play fair. Conduct training and competition within the rules.
3. Understand the basics of skill development and training methods appropriate for the level of your athletes. Learn and stay informed about coaching based on the principles of growth and development.
4. Follow the safety guidelines of your sport's National Governing Body.
5. Teach sportsmanship by example; make sure players feel good about doing their best, regardless of winning or losing. Never ridicule or shout at players for making mistakes or for losing.
6. Balance constructive criticism with support and praise.
7. Ensure that equipment and the facility are safe.
8. Educate athletes about the dangers of nutritional and substance abuse.

PRESEASON MEDICAL EXAMINATION

A preseason medical examination is a comprehensive medical evaluation performed by a qualified physician prior to any participation in a sport to determine an athlete's ability to train and compete.

Coaches and administrators should note that there are two types of preseason medical evaluations. The general physical evaluation is used by many scholastic or recreational programs in which athletes participate in several sports or only on a limited basis. The specialized medical evaluation is for athletes who compete at higher levels, which involves a more advanced and detailed screening.

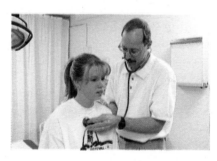

A general medical evaluation should be thorough and focus on broad health issues, including reviews of past problems and conditions related to family medical histories. The more specific medical evaluation should include an examination of specific performance-related skills and the athlete's medical capability to perform them, such as strength and flexibility tests and tightness in highly used muscle groups.

Importance for Athletes

An appropriate medical examination helps assess overall health, reveal past and present injuries that might be aggravated by participation in the sport, and identify conditions that could result in injuries. When preexisting conditions or injuries are found, treatment can be prescribed to heal the injury or alleviate the condition before training begins.

Guidelines for the Medical Approval/Examination

1. When possible, have athletes schedule examinations 4 to 6 weeks before the first practice so that any current injuries or physical problems can be addressed and, if needed, to permit referrals to specialists.
2. Suggest that athletes be examined by their primary care physician (if they have one) or another physician who is familiar with their medical history. It is desirable to use a physician who is familiar with sports medicine.
3. Ensure that the examining physician knows in which sport the athletes will be participating.
4. Require that the medical examination include a thorough and up-to-date medical history that addresses the following:
   - Previous injuries
   - Allergies
   - Medications
   - Hospitalizations
   - Operations
   - Immunizations
   - Family heart conditions
   - Skin conditions
   - Cold or heat sensitivities
   - Dietary habits
   - Eating disorders
   - Real or perceived weight problems
   - Use of anabolic steroids and other drugs
5. Specify that medical examinations evaluate the following:
   - General cardiovascular, musculoskeletal, and nutritional health
   - Fitness for the specific sport
   - Existing injuries
   - Conditions that might result in injuries

> Conditions that might limit or prevent participation in specific sports

6. Direct physicians to discuss with the athletes the completed evaluation, any unsafe practices (e.g., drug use), and dietary guidelines.
7. Ask for written notification of any problems or special conditions.
8. Ensure that the medical examination meets all legal and insurance requirements.
9. Require an annual examination for all athletes and more frequent examinations for athletes with chronic problems or athletes who are changing sports.
10. Require that the physician state in writing that there are no medical reasons to limit, restrict, or prohibit the athlete from participating.

EMERGENCY ACTION PLAN

An Emergency Action Plan is a written plan that every program and facility should have to prepare for potential emergencies. Certain types of emergencies, such as specific natural disasters, are more likely in some locations than in others. Emergencies, however, can occur anywhere. In addition to injuries, emergencies may include illnesses, such as heart attack, seizure, or stroke. Emergencies can result from a specific problem, such as fire, power failure, chemical spills, violent winds, tornadoes, lightning, earthquake, mudslides, or sudden flooding.

The facility's Emergency Action Plans should address all relevant categories of emergencies. Such plans should define the responsibility of everyone who may be involved, covering areas such as those following.

▶ Content of an Emergency Action Plan
- ➤ Layout
  - EMS personnel access and entry/exit routes
  - Location of rescue and first aid equipment
  - Location of telephones, with emergency telephone numbers posted
  - Location of keys to reach telephones or equipment
  - Exits and evacuation routes
- ➤ Equipment
  - Rescue equipment
  - First aid supplies
  - Emergency equipment (flashlights, fire extinguisher, etc.)
- ➤ Support Personnel
  - Within facility
    - Coaches
    - Athletic trainers
    - Athletic officials and referees
    - Facility administrators
    - Management personnel
    - Teachers
    - School nurse/physician
    - Athletic director
    - Clerical personnel
    - Maintenance personnel
  - External (provide telephone numbers)
    - EMS personnel
    - Police
    - Fire
    - Hazardous materials (Hazmat) team
    - Poison Control Center
    - Hospitals
    - Power and gas companies
    - Health department

➤ Staff Responsibilities
  • Assign each staff member a duty:
  • Person(s) to provide care
  • Person(s) to control bystanders and supervise other athletes
  • Person(s) to meet EMS personnel
  • Person(s) to transport injured athlete when appropriate
➤ Communication
  • How and when to call 9-1-1 or the local emergency number
  • Chain of command
  • Person to contact family/guardian
  • Person to deal with media
➤ Follow-up
  • Complete appropriate documentation (incident report, accident report, etc.)
  • Replace equipment and supplies
  • Emergency Action Plan evaluation
  • Staff debriefing
  • Critical Incident Stress Debriefing (if necessary)
  • Check on condition of injured athlete

CHECKING THE FACILITY AREA

Although facility managers, school departments, and other building owners and operators have certain responsibilities for providing a safe environment for training and competing, coaches are responsible for ensuring that locker rooms, workout rooms, gymnasiums, equipment, fields, and courses are safe. Coaches also should ensure that proper emergency care and safety equipment is available and accessible.

Importance for Athletes

A safe environment for training and competing can considerably reduce the incidence of athletic injuries.

Guidelines To Provide a Safe Environment

1. Regularly and thoroughly inspect all building areas, pools, equipment, fields, courses, and other playing surfaces used by your athletes.
2. Inspect potentially dangerous equipment (e.g., ropes, guide lines, trampolines), heavy-use equipment (e.g., playing surfaces, sleds, watercraft), and protective equipment (e.g., helmets, pads, guards) much more frequently.
3. Ensure that unused equipment is not stored in or dangerously close to a playing area.
4. Ensure that wall-mounted devices that could cause injury are padded and light bulbs have protective coverings.
5. During extreme weather (e.g., rain, high wind, ice), inspect equipment and fields, courses, and other outside playing surfaces, including support structures (e.g., tents, trailers), that could become unsafe.
6. Work with athletes to develop responsibility and respect for equipment.

7. Ask athletes to report any unsafe conditions related to the facility, pools, equipment, fields, courses, and other playing surfaces.
8. Know the maintenance techniques and schedules for the facility, pool, fields, courses, and other playing surfaces, and make sure they are enforced.
9. Report in writing damage to the facility, pools, fields, and courses, and request to have it repaired. Inspect repairs when completed.
10. Know the maintenance/replacement techniques and schedules for equipment.
11. Report in writing serious damage to equipment, and make sure that worn, damaged, or broken equipment is repaired, replaced, or not used.
12. Prevent athletes from using unsafe building areas, pools, equipment, fields, courses, and other playing surfaces. In particular, remove unsafe equipment immediately to prevent inadvertent or prohibited use.
13. Ensure adequate fluid replacement for athletes during all practices and competitions.
14. Ensure easy access to emergency equipment and first aid supplies.
15. Ensure telephone or radio access to enable contact with emergency medical services.

EQUIPMENT SELECTION AND USE

The coach is responsible for determining what equipment will be used in training and competing, regardless of the supplier, selecting appropriate equipment, making sure that equipment is available, overseeing the use of equipment, and ensuring that equipment is properly maintained and replaced when needed. Never modify equipment without consulting with and obtaining written agreement from the manufacturer. Any modifications to equipment may void equipment warranties and create liability concerns.

Importance for Athletes

Proper equipment can protect athletes from injury or reduce the severity of injury if one occurs, as well as enhance performance. To maximize injury prevention, equipment must be—

➤ Available.
➤ Appropriate.
➤ High-quality.
➤ In good condition.
➤ Sized properly.
➤ Fitted correctly.
➤ Used.
➤ Maintained.
➤ Repaired or replaced when damaged.

Guidelines for Equipment Selection and Use

1. Be knowledgeable about the different types of equipment available, including new developments in equipment materials and design.
2. Deal only with reputable suppliers and authorized dealers.
3. Provide quality equipment that is appropriate for the sport and size, strength, and skill level of the user.

4. Ensure athletes' safety by requiring the use of helmets, eye protection, mouth guards, and other critical safety equipment where appropriate.
5. Ensure that equipment meets all required codes or standards.
6. Understand equipment liability.
7. Have enough equipment on hand so that every athlete has access to appropriate equipment.
8. Inspect all new equipment for quality and defects before use.
9. Inspect all equipment—both that belonging to the athlete and that provided to the athlete—for wear at the beginning of each season. Be cautious of hand-me- down equipment.
10. During the season, inspect equipment periodically for wear and damage.
11. Know how to size equipment. Always follow manufacturers' recommendations.
12. Instruct athletes on the proper use, fit, cleaning, and maintenance of equipment.
13. Warn athletes about any dangers associated with equipment use.
14. Establish clear rules for equipment use and care and penalties for misuse.
15. Ensure proper care and use of equipment.
16. Establish a schedule for cleaning and maintaining equipment, especially shared equipment (e.g., batting helmets).
17. Have equipment repaired or replaced when needed.
18. Instruct athletes to report equipment damage.
19. Direct athletes to repair or replace their personal equipment when necessary.
20. Do not allow athletes to use unsafe equipment.
21. Maintain proper documentation regarding inventory, assignments to athletes, and inspections and maintenance of equipment.

SUPERVISING ATHLETES

Coaches are responsible for providing appropriate supervision to prevent unnecessary risk of injury. Coaches use two types of supervision. General supervision is the oversight of all areas and events taking place during the session, whether training or competition. Specific supervision is the oversight of specific elements or skills being performed. For the coach, this balance is important for protecting the health of athletes, since as the level of specific supervision increases (often targeted at a single athlete), the level of general supervision often decreases. The coach must continue to be aware of the activities of all athletes present.

Guidelines for Appropriate Supervision

A coach's supervision responsibilities start when the **first** athlete arrives at the sport facility and do not end until the **last** athlete leaves.

1. Consider athletes' maturity, age, size, weight, conditioning, and skill when determining the degree of supervision required.
2. Supervise athletes in all activities related to the sport:
   ➤ Traveling to and from training and competition, when appropriate
   ➤ Staying overnight

- ➤ Eating meals
- ➤ Dressing, assembling equipment, and otherwise preparing for training and competition
- ➤ Warming up
- ➤ Training and competing
- ➤ Cooling down
- ➤ Putting equipment away, showering, and otherwise concluding training and competition
- ➤ Receiving treatment for injuries
3. Act quickly and decisively to correct conditions and actions that could lead to injury or damage.
4. Properly plan and direct activities.
5. Increase the level of specific supervision as the risk of injury increases.
6. Insist that athletes use appropriate training techniques.
7. Ensure that athletes use equipment safely.
8. Make sure that athletes use facilities, fields, and courses safely.
9. Be alert to conditions that require additional supervision.
10. Be alert to changing conditions that could increase the risk of injury.
11. Increase the level of supervision when athletes are learning new techniques or equipment.
12. Do not delegate authority unless you are positive that discipline and control will be maintained.
13. Be accessible to athletes and other coaches.

Guidelines for Parents

If parents are involved in your sports activities, parental action—or inaction—can play a significant role in preventing or lessening the severity of injuries. Coaches must clearly and firmly communicate to parents how they can help and harm athletes and what their role should be.

Importance for Athletes

Supportive parents can assist athletes in their training and competition, as well as help them maintain their psychological fitness.

Guidelines for Working Effectively with Parents

1. Develop an understanding and supportive working relationship with parents, families, and agents.
2. At the beginning of each season, clearly communicate the following either with a face-to-face parent orientation or by distributing a fact sheet:
   ➤ Medical requirements (e.g., the preseason medical examination)
   ➤ What the sport entails (for younger athletes)
   ➤ The physical demands on the athletes
   ➤ The psychological demands on the athletes
   ➤ The potential for injury
   ➤ Your coaching philosophy and methods
   ➤ Your goals for the season
   ➤ The importance or lack of importance of winning/losing
   ➤ The need to learn from mistakes
   ➤ How athletes are chosen to participate
   ➤ The vast differences in athletes' developmental and skill levels
   ➤ Boys and girls competing together (if applicable)
   ➤ The training schedule—formal practice and practice at home (if applicable)
   ➤ Schedule of competitive events
   ➤ Equipment requirements, cost, and where to get it
   ➤ Nutritional requirements
   ➤ Dangers and signals of nutritional abuse and eating disorders

- ➤ The need for support, but not pressure
- ➤ The dangers of competitive stress
- ➤ The importance of rest
- ➤ Guidelines for parent behavior during competition (p. 13)
- ➤ How to contact you

3. Encourage parents, family members, and agents to talk with you about any of their questions or concerns.

4. As appropriate, involve parents as assistant coaches, equipment managers, drivers, phone-chain managers, etc.

5. Specify acceptable parental behavior at competitive events:
   - ➤ Stay in the spectator area.
   - ➤ Remain seated (if applicable).
   - ➤ Do not coach from the sidelines.
   - ➤ Do not make derogatory comments about any athletes, parents, or officials.
   - ➤ Do not advise, criticize, or otherwise interfere with the coach.

6. Direct parents, family members, and agents to closely monitor athletes' medical needs and report any concerns, particularly—
   - ➤ Overexertion.
   - ➤ Overuse.
   - ➤ Stress.

PREVENTING FURTHER INJURY

When injuries occur, coaches must act quickly and decisively to prevent further injury.

Importance for Athletes

Correcting unsafe conditions helps provide a safe environment for training and competing.

Guidelines for Preventing Further Injury

1. Review programs and survey the environment to identify the cause or causes of injuries and take corrective actions.
2. Establish a written record of the corrective actions taken.
3. When appropriate, review the injury, the causes, and the corrective actions with your athletes and other members of the coaching staff.

INJURY PREVENTION CHECKLIST

Ensure that all the following safety steps have been taken before the season begins, during training and competition, and after the season ends.

▶ *Before the Season*

___ Update policies and regulations
___ Medical examination/approval
___ Parental permission forms signed
___ Team/group matching (size, skill)
___ Preseason conditioning
___ Training program preparation
   ___ Staff skill training
   ___ Instructional materials
   ___ Practice plans
___ Emergency Action Plans
___ First aid kit stocked and available
___ Emergency numbers
___ *Sport Safety Training Handbook*
___ All coaches properly trained and certified
___ Proper orientations arranged for new coaches
___ Facility inspection
___ Equipment inspection
___ Communication equipment available, with backup system available

___ Parent orientation program (if applicable)
___ Athlete orientation
  ___ Risks
  ___ Safety procedures
  ___ Injury prevention
  ___ Changes in rules, techniques, or equipment
  ___ Equipment use and maintenance
    instruction
  ___ Facility use instructions
  ___ Documentation that athletes have been oriented

▶*During Training and Competition*
___ Training program assessment and revision
___ General supervision
  ___ Program implementation
  ___ Equipment use
  ___ Environment (heat, cold, hazardous weather)
___ Periodic facility inspection and maintenance
___ (document dates and results)
___ Periodic equipment inspection and
  maintenance (document dates and results)

▶ *After the Season*
___ Off-season conditioning
___ Program assessment and revision
___ Staff skill training assessment
___ Injury cause and response evaluation
___ Facility inspection
___ Equipment inspection

▼ PREVENTING SPECIFIC INJURIES

HEAD, NECK, AND BACK INJURIES

Follow all injury prevention guidelines to help prevent
head, neck, and back injury. Should an injury involve the

head or spine, recognize the potential for serious injury and respond to prevent further injury to the spinal cord.

RECOGNIZING SPINAL INJURY

The way an injury occurred may give you some idea if a spinal injury is likely. Following are situations in which a spinal injury is possible:

➤ Any fall from higher than the person's height
➤ Any athlete found unconscious for an unknown reason
➤ Any significant head injury, especially with contact at the crown or forehead
➤ Any injury related to a diving board, water slide, or diving from a height (such as a bank or a cliff)
➤ Any dive into shallow water
➤ Any violent collision

In addition, look for the following signals of a possible head, neck, or back injury:

➤ Severe pain or pressure in the head, neck, or back
➤ Tingling or lack of sensation in the extremities
➤ Partial or complete loss of movement of any body part
➤ Unusual bumps or depressions on the head or neck
➤ Sudden memory loss
➤ Change in level of consciousness
➤ Persistent headache
➤ Blood or other fluids in the ears or nose
➤ Heavy external bleeding of the head, neck, or back
➤ Seizures
➤ Impaired speaking, vision, or breathing as a result of the injury
➤ Nausea or vomiting
➤ Loss of balance
➤ Bruising of the head, especially around the eyes or behind the ears

Guidelines to Prevent Spinal Injury

1. **Do not move the athlete** unless absolutely necessary.
2. Support the head and neck in the position in which the athlete was found.
3. Call 9-1-1 or the local emergency number and wait for EMS personnel to arrive.
4. If CPR is necessary, minimize movement of the head and neck by only lifting the chin (jaw thrust). Tilt the head back only to the extent necessary to get air into the lungs when the chin lift alone does not open the airway (see CPR, p. 110).
5. Provide additional care for the injury (see Head injuries, p. 123 and Back or neck injury, p. 68).

▼ MUSCULOSKELETAL INJURIES

WARM-UP/COOL-DOWN

Warm-up activities—slow, sustained stretching exercises, calisthenics, and slowly increasing the intensity of motion—prepare the body for training and competition, both physiologically and psychologically. Likewise, cool-down activities—light activity and stretching—help the body make the transition from vigorous activity to a normal state of activity.

Importance for Athletes

Warm-up:

Beginning a training session or competition without warming up greatly increases the chance of injury. A proper warm-up helps athletes train and compete without being injured by—

➤ Increasing body temperature.
➤ Increasing respiration (oxygen availability).
➤ Increasing heart rate.
➤ Reducing the risk of muscle and tendon strains by stretching tight muscles.
➤ Reducing the risk of ligament sprains.

Cool-down:

Blood and muscle lactic acid levels drop faster during active cool-down than during rest. Abruptly stopping intensive physical activity can result in muscle cramps, soreness, and stiffness and may increase the potential for fainting or dizziness caused by blood pooling. A proper cool-down enhances athletic activity by—

➤ Gradually reducing muscle workout intensity.
➤ Continuing the muscle-pump action to allow increased blood circulation while—
  • Reducing pooling of blood.
  • Helping remove wastes.

Guidelines for Warm-Up/Cool-Down Activities

Warm-up:

1. Inform athletes of the importance of properly warming up.
2. Teach athletes the warm-up activities to perform before training and competing:
   ➤ First, appropriate calisthenics (for strength) depending on the sport to raise body temperature

➤ Second, appropriate stretching exercises (for flexibility)
➤ Third, partial- and full-motion activities for each athlete's particular position or event, at varying speeds, distances, or intensities
3. Direct warm-up activities of athletes to ensure a slow increase in the intensity of motion, particularly the motion actually used in the sport.
4. Ensure that warm-up activities are tailored to each athlete's conditioning and position or event.
5. Ensure that athletes warm up for at least 10 minutes.
6. Ensure that warm-up activities do not cause fatigue.

Cool-down:
1. Inform athletes of the importance of properly cooling down the body after exercise.
2. Teach athletes the cool-down activities to perform after training and competing:
➤ First, partial- and full-motion activities for each athlete's particular position/event, at reduced speeds, distances, or intensities
➤ Second, light calisthenics
➤ Third, stretching exercises
3. Direct cool-down activities to ensure a gradual reduction of the intensity of activity.
4. Ensure that athletes perform the cool-down activity for at least 10 minutes.

TRAINING METHODS

Training methods and the type, frequency, duration, and intensity of training should vary among athletes, depending on the athlete's age, physical conditioning, mental state, and training goals. The purpose of training is to prepare for competition. Training is not disciplinary activity, unsupervised play, or competition itself.

Importance for Athletes

In addition to improving performance, appropriate training is an important element of injury prevention in all sports. Training that focuses on correct technique can help prevent both chronic and overuse injury.

Guidelines for Training

1. Ensure that training begins before the season starts so that athletes are in good condition for the first day of practice. Injuries are more likely when poorly conditioned athletes overtrain early in the season.
2. Ensure that training balances fitness and skill development in all training sessions.
3. Require proper warm-up (see Warm-up/Cool-down, p. 19).
4. Ensure that training intensity increases gradually. Trying to progress too rapidly often leads to injury.
5. Increase training time, distance, or repetitions no more than 10 percent weekly.
6. Recognize the impact of cumulative training increases, such as simultaneous increases in duration, frequency, or intensity.
7. Teach athletes to be aware of their training levels.
8. Note athletes' changes in skill levels and techniques.
9. Encourage variation in athletic activities.

10. Use strength and weight training when appropriate, but only with proper instruction and supervision.
11. In warmer, more humid climates, modify training to prevent heat-related emergencies (p. 26).
12. Require proper cool-down (p. 21).

PREVENTING OVERUSE INJURIES

Overuse injuries—such as bursitis, shin splints, stress fractures, and tendinitis—generally are caused by repetitive stress and damage to tissue.

Overuse injuries generally occur more often in organized sports, as opposed to acute sports injuries, which occur in both play and organized activities. Primary contributing factors to overuse injuries include the following:

➤ Athletes in organized sports often overtrain or continue to participate when fatigued or injured.
➤ Coaches—most often volunteer amateurs coaching in youth programs—may be unaware of appropriate conditioning, training, and techniques.
➤ Athletes often fail to report injuries.
➤ Coaches fail to recognize the signals of overuse injuries.
➤ Young athletes are predisposed to overuse injuries because of the physiology of growing:
  • The growth cartilage of younger athletes is more easily damaged than the cartilage in older athletes.
  • Muscles and tendons of younger athletes tend to be tighter than in older athletes because of rapid bone growth.
➤ Young athletes specialize in a select sport or sports at too early an age.
➤ Athletes sometimes avoid sports with a high risk of acute injury (e.g., rugby) without properly understanding that overuse injuries can occur in seemingly safe sports (e.g., swimming).

Importance for Athletes

Severe overuse injuries can impact future sports participation and physical activities of any athlete. In general, young athletes are more susceptible to overuse injuries than older athletes, and these injuries to young athletes may have more serious long-term consequences than to older athletes. Fortunately, most overuse injuries can be prevented.

Risk factors for overuse injuries:
➤ Growth (younger athletes)
➤ Musculoskeletal weakness
➤ Malnutrition
➤ Obesity
➤ Rapid increases in training frequency, duration, or intensity
➤ Strength imbalances
➤ Flexibility imbalances
➤ Malalignment of legs
➤ Improper or ill-fitting footwear
➤ Hard playing surface
➤ Past injuries
➤ Inadequate rest or fatigue

Stages of overuse injuries:
➤ Initially, pain occurs only after the activity.
➤ Eventually, pain begins to occur during and after the activity.
➤ Later, pain occurs throughout the activity.
➤ Finally, pain occurs during sport and nonsport activities.

Guidelines to Prevent Overuse Injuries

1. Know the risk factors.
2. Improve training in proper technique for coaches, particularly amateur coaches.

3. Require sport-specific preparticipation physical examinations.
4. Develop fitness by increasing strength, flexibility, and endurance.
5. Encourage athletes to report pain and injuries.
6. Positively respond to athletes' complaints of pain.
7. Inform parents about general risk factors, sport-specific stress areas, and the signals of overuse injuries.
8. Increase training time, distance, and repetitions no more than 10 percent a week.

▼ OTHER EMERGENCIES

PREVENTING HEAT-RELATED EMERGENCIES

Heat-related emergencies, or hyperthermia, may be life threatening. Heat stroke, heat exhaustion, and heat cramps result from the body losing so much fluid that its natural cooling mechanism fails and the body overheats. Conditions contributing to heat-related emergencies include—

➤ Hot environmental conditions.
➤ High humidity.
➤ Extreme physical exertion.
➤ Inappropriately layered or rubberized clothing.
➤ Inadequate fluid intake.

Importance for Athletes

Heat-related emergencies may result in illness, shock, and even death. Fortunately, *heat-related emergencies are preventable.*

In general, younger athletes are more susceptible to heat-related emergencies than older athletes:

➤ Children do not cool naturally in hot weather as effectively as adults.

➤ Children are slower to adjust to hot conditions than adults.
➤ Children often do not instinctively replenish fluids.

Guidelines to Prevent Heat-Related Emergencies

1. Schedule practice during cooler times of the day.
2. Use appropriate equipment. When appropriate, instruct athletes to—
   ➤ Wear net-type jerseys.
   ➤ Wear T-shirts and shorts, not pads (if applicable).
   ➤ Remove helmets (if applicable) when not playing/scrimmaging.
   ➤ Avoid wearing sweat suits.
   ➤ Change sweat-soaked clothing.
3. Be certain athletes are fully hydrated *before* practice and competition.
4. Schedule and enforce frequent water breaks.
5. Do not use salt tablets.
6. Reduce or cancel practice when the weather is excessively hot or humid.
7. When athletes are practicing or competing, allow time for adjustment to warmer climates.

PREVENTING COLD-RELATED EMERGENCIES

Cold-related emergencies include frostbite and hypothermia. Hypothermia is a condition in which the body's warming mechanisms cannot maintain normal body temperature and the body cools. Contributing factors for body cooling include air temperature, humidity, wind, and the condition of the skin (wet or dry). Frostbite is the freezing of local skin or body areas. Hypothermia and frostbite may occur together or separately.

Importance for Athletes

Outdoor sports in cool or cold weather, particularly those in or around snow, ice, or water, place athletes at risk for frostbite or hypothermia. Hypothermia is generally caused by prolonged exposure to wet, windy, and cold environments. Frostbite may occur as a result of being underdressed for the weather conditions or simply remaining in the cold too long without adequate protection.

Hypothermia may be a life-threatening medical emergency. Frostbite may result in disability or loss of body tissue.

Guidelines to Prevent Hypothermia

1. Do not start an activity in, on, or around cold water unless you know you can get help quickly in an emergency.
2. Be aware of the wind chill.
3. Dress appropriately and avoid staying in the cold too long.
4. Drink plenty of warm fluids or water.
5. Avoid caffeine and alcohol.
6. Stay active to maintain body heat.
7. Take frequent breaks from the cold.
8. Wear a Coast Guard-approved life jacket while boating. Have life jackets on hand whenever you are near cold water. A life jacket will help you float in a rescue position if you fall into cold water, and some styles provide insulation against cold water.
9. If you are near water in cold weather, wear rain gear or wool clothes. Wool insulates you even when it is wet. Wear layers of clothing and wear a hat. As much as 60 percent of body heat loss occurs through the head.

10. Carry matches in a waterproof container. You may need to build a fire to warm up after a fall into cold water.
11. Carry a chocolate bar or high-energy food containing sugar. Sugar stimulates shivering, the body's internal mechanism for rewarming itself.

Guidelines to Prevent Frostbite

1. Dress appropriately and avoid staying in the cold too long. Wear a hat and layers of clothing.
2. Avoid unnecessary exposure of any part of the body to the cold.
3. Drink plenty of warm fluids or water.
4. Avoid caffeine and alcohol.
5. Take frequent breaks from the cold.
6. Get out of the cold immediately if the signals of frostbite appear: skin that appears waxy, is cold to the touch, or is discolored (flushed, white, yellow, blue). Give care (p. 122).

PREVENTING WEATHER-RELATED INJURIES

Weather conditions may affect the safety of athletes in all outdoor and even indoor activities. Since weather conditions vary greatly in different parts of the United States, you should know what conditions to be aware of at your facility and follow your facility's weather-related guidelines.

Importance for Athletes

Weather-related injuries include being struck by lightning or being injured by hail or debris from high winds, tornadoes, or other storm conditions. **Lightning strikes are one of the leading causes of death for children under age 10 in organized sports.** These injuries can easily be prevented. Take weather conditions seriously.

Guidelines to Prevent Weather-Related Injuries

1. Pay attention to weather forecasts, and monitor weather reports, particularly with changing weather patterns.
2. If far from a weatherproof shelter, watch cloud patterns and conditions for signals of an approaching storm.
3. Move athletes to a safe location at the first sound of thunder.
4. In a storm, keep everyone away from windows. Injuries may occur from flying debris or glass if the window breaks.
5. Do not let anyone shower during a thunderstorm. Water and metal are both excellent conductors of electricity.
6. Do not use the telephone except for emergencies.
7. If caught outdoors and there is not enough time to reach a safe building—
   ➤ Keep away from structures in open areas, such as picnic shelters and dugouts.
   ➤ Keep away from tall, isolated trees or objects that project above the landscape.
   ➤ Keep away from water and grounded objects, such as metal fences, metal bleachers, tanks, rails, and pipes.
8. If there is a tornado alert, go to the location specified in the facility's Emergency Action Plan. This may be the basement or the lowest interior level of a building.
9. Wait at least 15 minutes after thunder and lightning stop entirely before allowing athletes to return outdoors. Continue to watch for approaching storms and monitor weather forecasts.
10. In indoor facilities, changes in outdoor conditions, particularly those that are unseasonable, may affect

facility conditions (e.g., warmer temperatures and increased humidity). Be aware of these situations because athletes accustomed to a cooler indoor temperature may sweat more, resulting in a less secure grip on equipment or more perspiration on floor surfaces.

PREVENTING DEHYDRATION

Dehydration occurs when athletes fail to drink enough liquids to replace fluids lost through perspiration or urine output. Other causes include—

➤ Inadequate fluid intake.
➤ Profuse sweating.
➤ Reduced electrolyte intake, such as potassium found in some foods (e.g., fruit) and fluids.
➤ Injection of hypertonic solutions, such as intravenous solutions while under medical care.
➤ Ingestion of diuretic substances (e.g., salt, caffeine).

Importance for Athletes

Dehydrated athletes do not perform well. Fluid loss through sweating directly impacts strength, endurance, power, and cognitive abilities. Excessive fluid loss may cause an athlete to feel fatigued, weak, irritable, nauseous, dizzy, and even disoriented.

Guidelines to Prevent Dehydration

1. 2 to 3 hours before a workout or competition: Drink 2 cups of fluid.
2. 1 hour before a workout or competition: Drink 1 cup of fluid.
3. 15 minutes before a workout or competition: Drink 1/2 cup of fluid.

4. Before a workout or competition: Weigh each athlete.
5. Every 10 to 20 minutes during a workout or competition: Drink 1/2 cup of fluid.
6. After a workout or competition: Weigh each athlete and drink 2 cups of fluid for every pound of weight lost.

Guidelines for Rehydration

1. Drink large amounts at one time.
2. Drink cool fluids, such as water.
3. Drink 4 8-ounce glasses of fluid for every 1000 calories expended.

PREVENTING NUTRITIONAL ABUSE AND EATING DISORDERS

Nutritional abuse and eating disorders are a significant problem in sports. They include—

➤ Anorexia nervosa: An intense fear of becoming fat that tends to increase with weight loss. Refusal to maintain normal weight. Most often affects teenage women but has also occurred in male athletes. Also related to extreme dieting by athletes trying to "make weight."

➤ Bulimia: A neurotic disorder characterized by heavy overeating followed by forced vomiting,

31

fasting, or induced diarrhea. Most often occurs in adolescents and young-adult women.

➤ Eating to bulk: Eating simply to add weight, often without proper physical training.

➤ Poor nutrition: Eating improper foods due to poor eating habits, ignorance of good nutrition, or poverty.

➤ Compulsive overeating.

Anorexia and bulimia are true psychological illnesses with physical symptoms and must be treated by professional personnel, including psychologists, physicians, and nutritionists.

Importance for Athletes

Proper nutrition and normal eating habits are extremely important for athletes' ability to train and compete, as well as for athletes' general health, resistance to and recovery from injury and illness, normal growth and development, and long-term well-being. Importantly, nutritional abuse and eating disorders may be signals of emotional problems, such as those related to competitive stress, self-image, and self-esteem.

Nutritional abuse and eating disorders may result in undernourishment and dehydration. In particular, obese athletes are prone to hypertension, diabetes, cardiovascular conditions, and heat exhaustion, as well as psychological problems associated with being overweight.

Signals of common eating disorders:

➤ Anorexia
- Rapid weight loss
- Dieting although thin
- Poor self-image
- Belief that body is fat (even when underweight)
- Menstrual period stops
- Unusual interest in food
- Strange eating rituals
- Eating in secret
- Obsession with exercise
- Depression

➤ Bulimia
- Menstrual period stops
- Unusual interest in food
- Strange eating rituals
- Eating in secret
- Obsession with exercise
- Depression
- Binging (often without weight gain)
- Purging (vomiting, diarrhea, exercise)
- Spending large amounts of time in the bathroom (to vomit)
- Substance abuse

➤ Eating to bulk/compulsive overeating
- Aggressive weight gain (generally fat over muscle)
- Obsession with food
- Consumption of large amounts of junk food

➤ Poor nutrition
- Malnutrition
  - Unusually fatigued
  - Heat-related emergencies
  - Frequent injuries
- Obesity

Eating disorders may become life threatening! The National Institutes of Health estimate that 10 percent of people with eating disorders die from starvation, cardiac arrest, or suicide.

Guidelines to Prevent Nutritional Abuse and Eating Disorders

1. Understand basic factors about eating disorders:
   - ➤ Athletes with eating disorders often deny their problem and refuse help.
   - ➤ The earlier treatment begins, the greater the chance of full recovery.
   - ➤ Treatment can be life saving.
2. Provide athletes with accurate, credible, up-to-date, and relevant nutritional information.
3. Discuss nutritional abuse and eating disorders with parents.
4. Use caution when relating weight to performance. Seek advice from a trained nutritionist rather than suggesting dieting or weight increase.
5. Use caution when discussing weight or body fat with athletes. Seek advice from a sports psychologist or nutritionist to avoid triggering eating disorders in athletes.
6. Seek expert advice if you notice rapid weight loss with any athlete.
7. Advise athletes who are dieting to seek medical nutritional advice: Stringent dieting can trigger eating disorders.
8. Discuss the hazards of bulking up and discourage the practice.
9. Seek expert advice for athletes who experience rapid weight increase.
10. Advise athletes who are attempting to increase weight to seek help from a physician, qualified trainer, or dietician.

11. Discuss athletes' diets with them frequently to ensure that they are eating regular meals, that their diets are properly balanced, and that they are not developing poor eating habits.
12. Try to schedule practices so that athletes can eat meals with their families.
13. Encourage athletes to drink fluids—especially water—continuously during training and competition, not only when thirsty.
14. Discourage athletes from eating candy for sugar highs.
15. Dispel the myth of the pregame meal: Athletes should eat only easily digestible, high-carbohydrate, low-fat foods before competition—never high-protein, high-fat foods, such as steaks.
16. Direct athletes to eat a balanced meal soon after training and competition.
17. Direct athletes' specific diet-related questions to nutrition professionals.

ALLERGIC REACTIONS

Severe allergic reactions are rare. But when one occurs, it is truly a life-threatening medical emergency. A severe allergic reaction, called anaphylaxis, is a form of shock. It can be caused by an insect bite or sting or by contact with drugs, medications, foods, or chemicals.

Importance for Athletes

An athlete with known allergies typically knows what to avoid and does so. The athlete may have a medical kit to treat an allergic reaction. Not all allergies are known by the athlete or can be prevented, however, so it is important to recognize the first signals of an allergic reaction and seek medical help immediately to prevent the problem from worsening.

Elite athletes should not take prescription or over-the-counter medication without first checking to see if it contains banned substances. See p. 40 for the USOC Drug Hotline.

Signals of Allergic Reaction

➤ Reaction occurs suddenly, within seconds or minutes after contact with the substance.
➤ Skin or body area in contact with the substance usually swells and turns red. Hives, itching, and rash may occur.
➤ Breathing difficulty is common, including coughing and wheezing.
➤ Other signals are weakness, nausea, vomiting, dizziness, sneezing, and bloodshot, swollen eyes.

See p. 66 for the care for someone having an allergic reaction.

EXERCISE-INDUCED ASTHMA

Exercise-induced asthma is a medical condition that occurs when exercising causes swollen tissue to obstruct the airway, resulting in breathing difficulty, and sometimes, coughing, chest pain, chest tightness, or wheezing. Note that younger athletes may have exercise-induced asthma that has not been diagnosed and of which they are unaware. Do not assume that an athlete with breathing difficulty is simply "out of shape"; any athlete who seems to have unusual breathing difficulty should be medically evaluated.

Importance for Athletes

When not cared for properly, exercise-induced asthma may have a serious effect on an athlete. Fortunately, with most asthmatic athletes, the asthma may be controlled, allowing the athlete to train and compete with minimal discomfort or interference. *Asthmatic athletes should not be discouraged from participating in sports.*

Guidelines to Prevent Exercise-Induced Asthma

1. Understand exercise-induced asthma.
   ➤ Even asthma that is normally well controlled can cause airway obstruction after exercise.
   ➤ The likelihood of exercise-induced asthma attacks depends on a number of factors, including—
      • The athlete's health.
      • How well the asthmatic condition is controlled.
      • The intensity of exercise.
      • The length of exercise.
      • Stress.
   ➤ Cold, dry air and many airborne pollutants increase airway obstruction.
2. Medication may be needed prior to training or competing.
3. A customized warm-up may be needed for an athlete who experiences exercise-induced asthma.
4. Because conditioning improves breathing efficiency, better conditioned athletes in general will have a lower incidence of exercise-induced asthma.

PREVENTING SUBSTANCE ABUSE

From youth sports through professional competition, abuse of recreational drugs (including alcohol and tobacco products) and performance-enhancing substances (such as anabolic steroids) has become a significant problem. As a result, coaches need to recognize the signals of substance abuse and intervene promptly and effectively when substance abuse is suspected or known.

Importance for Athletes

Substance abuse—whether with recreational drugs or performance-enhancing drugs—may have a detrimental impact on an athlete's performance, career, and lifestyle. Substance abuse may have serious long-term negative physical and mental side effects. Substance abuse also may result in an athlete being banned from athletic competition.

General signals of substance abuse include—
➤ Abnormal behavior.
➤ Mood swings.
➤ Argumentativeness.
➤ Resisting authority.
➤ Deceitfulness.
➤ Changes in appearance.
➤ Abrupt weight change.
➤ Stretch marks.
➤ Obsessive attention to body.
➤ Changes in performance.
➤ Altered concentration.
➤ Habitually early or late arrival at practice.
➤ High incidence of injuries.
➤ Heavy use of medication.
➤ Needle marks.

The use of anabolic steroids, growth hormones, stimulants, and other performance-enhancing substances cheats honest athletes. It may also be life threatening.

Use of anabolic steroids increases the risk of—

➤ Heart attack.
➤ Heart disease.
➤ Stroke.
➤ Kidney disease.
➤ Hepatitis.
➤ Liver tumors.

Side effects of anabolic steroids in men:
➤ Breast development
➤ Shrunken testicles
➤ Impotence
➤ Excessive acne

Side effects of anabolic steroids in women:
➤ Breast shrinkage
➤ Clitoral enlargement
➤ Infertility
➤ Male-pattern baldness
➤ Deepened voice
➤ Excessive acne

Side effects of anabolic steroids in children:
➤ Possible impairment of growth
➤ Possible impairment of development

Side effects of growth hormone:
➤ Bone deformity
➤ Glucose intolerance
➤ Hypertension
➤ Heart disease

Side effects of stimulants:
➤ Headaches
➤ Heart palpitations
➤ Hypertension
➤ Insomnia
➤ Nervousness

Guidelines to Prevent Substance Abuse

1. Take the initiative in dealing with substance abuse and make it part of your athletic program.
   Become—and stay—well informed about substance abuse:
   ➤ Causes
   ➤ Signals

- ➤ Dangers
- ➤ Intervention techniques
2. Become knowledgeable about performance-enhancing substances:
   - ➤ Steroids
   - ➤ Growth hormones
   - ➤ Blood doping
3. Know which drugs are banned for athletes:
   - ➤ Illegal substances
   - ➤ Ingredients of supplements
   - ➤ Over-the-counter medications (such as cold medicine and eye drops)
   - ➤ To find out if a substance is banned, call the U.S. Olympic Committee Drug Hotline: 1-800-233-0393
4. Know which drugs are approved for training but not for competition.
5. Understand urine testing procedures.
6. Be aware of techniques for masking drug use.
7. Insist that all members of the coaching staff—assistant coaches, trainers, team doctors, and volunteers—learn about substance abuse, banned drugs, and drug testing. Contact your sport's National Governing Body for more information.
8. Keep continuously alert to the signals of substance abuse—both recreational drugs and performance-enhancing substances.
9. Provide effective, credible information to athletes on the use and abuse of recreational drugs (including alcohol and tobacco products):
   - ➤ Types of illegal or inappropriate recreational drugs
   - ➤ Side effects
   - ➤ Legal consequences
   - ➤ Penalties as an athlete
   - ➤ Signals

10. Provide effective, credible information to athletes and parents on the use of steroids, growth hormones, and blood doping:
    ➤ Banned drugs
    ➤ Signals of steroid use
    ➤ Side effects
    ➤ Penalties
    ➤ Ethical consequences
    ➤ Drug testing
11. Address personal prejudices about substance abuse that may prevent you from discussing it objectively.
12. If you choose to intervene when responding to substance abuse or the suspicion of substance abuse—
    ➤ Carefully and privately document your suspicions.
    ➤ If necessary, obtain assistance from a professional experienced with substance abuse.
    ➤ If you talk to an athlete about possible substance abuse, do so privately and express concern about the athlete's health and well-being.
    ➤ If rehabilitation is needed, rely on professionals.

PSYCHOLOGICAL INJURIES

The stress to train rigorously and compete at a high level may result in psychological injuries—with both mental and physical signals—in athletes of all ages and in all sports. Stress may be caused by competition, coaches, parents, or teammates or may be self-imposed by the athlete.

Importance for Athletes

Psychological injuries caused by stress may have a significant and long-lasting impact on athletic activities and lifestyle. In the short term, psychological injuries may leave athletes emotionally unable to train and compete and may cause serious physical problems. In the long term, psychological injuries may affect athletes' self-esteem and quality of life.

Signals of stress:

➤ Muscle aches, pain, and stiffness
➤ Headaches
➤ Nausea
➤ Rashes
➤ Fatigue
➤ Inability to sleep
➤ Acute anxiety
➤ Hyperactivity
➤ Decrease in quality of school work (student)
➤ Poor job performance
➤ Eating disorders
➤ Depression

Guidelines to Prevent Psychological Injuries

1. To prevent burnout, limit the amount of time during and outside the season that athletes can train without taking time away from the sport.
2. Use a coaching style that is appropriate for the age, experience, and ability of athletes.
3. Ensure that the size, maturity, and skill level of athletes are comparable.
4. Create an environment for training and competition that is fun and encourages sportsmanship.
5. Develop a training program that offers variety rather than repetition.
6. Be flexible.
7. Do not overemphasize the importance of winning.
8. Keep individual and team goals in perspective.
9. Use positive reinforcement techniques to motivate athletes, particularly younger athletes.
10. Communicate to parents, family members, and agents the dangers of pushing young athletes too

hard, as well as the stress that may result from overzealous behavior during competition.

11. To the extent possible and warranted, provide for non-sport diversions, such as social events.

PREVENTING DISEASE TRANSMISSION WHEN GIVING CARE

Some people are concerned about the risk of infection as a result of giving care to an injured person. It is important for you to know how diseases are transmitted and how to protect yourself when giving first aid.

Diseases that can pass from one person to another are called infectious diseases. Infectious diseases develop when germs invade the body and cause illness. The most common germs are bacteria and viruses.

Bacteria can live outside the body and do not depend on other organisms for life. The number of bacteria that infect humans is very small. Some cause serious infections, but these can be treated with antibiotics.

Viruses depend on other organisms to live. Once in the body, they are more difficult to remove. Few medications can fight viruses. The body's immune system is the best protection against infection.

In first aid situations, diseases can be transmitted from one person to another by touching, breathing, and biting.

You can become infected if you touch an infected person and germs in that person's blood or other bodily fluids pass into your body through breaks or cuts in the skin or through the lining of your eyes, nose, and mouth. Therefore the greatest risk of infection occurs when you touch blood or other bodily fluids directly.

You can also be infected when you touch an object that has been soiled by a person's blood or bodily fluids. Be careful when handling soiled objects. Sharp objects can cut your skin and pass germs. Avoid touching blood and blood-soiled objects with your bare hands.

Some diseases, such as the common cold, are transmitted by air. It is possible to become infected if you breathe air exhaled by an infected person. Airborne infection can occur during sneezing, coughing, and so on. Most of us are exposed to germs everyday in our jobs, on the bus, or in a crowded restaurant. Fortunately, simply being exposed to these germs is usually not enough for diseases to be transmitted.

Some diseases are passed more easily than others. We all know how quickly the flu can pass from person to person at home or at work. Although these diseases can create discomfort, they are often temporary and are not serious to healthy adults.

Other diseases can be more serious, such as hepatitis B (HBV) and HIV, which causes AIDS. Although very serious, they are not easily transmitted and are not passed by casual contact, such as shaking hands. In a first aid setting, the primary way to transmit HBV or HIV is through blood-to-blood contact.

By following some basic guidelines, you can help reduce disease transmission when providing care. These are called **universal precautions:**

➤ Avoid contact with bodily fluids, such as blood, when possible.

➤ Place barriers, such as disposable latex/nitrile gloves, a clean dry cloth, or a face shield between the person's bodily fluids and yourself.

➤ Protect any cuts, scrapes, and openings on both you and the injured person's skin by wearing protective clothing, such as latex/nitrile gloves.

➤ Wash your hands with soap and water immediately before and after providing care, even if you wear gloves.

➤ Do not eat, drink, or touch your mouth, nose, or eyes when providing care.

➤ Do not touch objects that may be soiled with blood, mucus, or other bodily substances. These items must be disposed of properly to prevent others from coming in contact with them.

Following these guidelines significantly decreases your risk of contracting or transmitting an infectious disease. Remember always to provide care in ways that protect you and the injured or ill person from disease transmission.

PREVENTING HIV TRANSMISSION

AIDS stands for acquired immunodeficiency syndrome. It is caused by the human immunodeficiency virus (HIV). When the virus gets into the body, it damages the immune system. About half the people with HIV develop AIDS within 10 years after being infected. People infected with HIV may not feel or appear sick and may not even know that they are infected. Eventually, the weakened immune system makes the body vulnerable to certain other types of infections.

The HIV virus enters the body in three ways:

1. Through blood-to-blood contact, such as by sharing a needle or syringe
2. Through the mucous membranes lining body openings, such as the rectum and vagina, as may occur by having oral, anal, or vaginal sex with an HIV-infected person without using a latex condom
3. From mother to infant during pregnancy or birth or while breast-feeding

Since 1985, all donated blood in the United States has been tested for signs of HIV. As a result, the risk of HIV infection from a blood transfusion is extremely low.

Unless broken or cut, the skin helps to protect against HIV infection. There are no documented cases of HIV having been transmitted by saliva, urine, feces, vomit, or tears.

The likelihood of HIV transmission during a first aid situation is very low. Always give care in ways that protect you and the injured person from disease transmission. Following the universal precautions listed on p. 44 will help prevent the transmission of HIV.

If you think you may be at risk for HIV infection, you are encouraged to seek medical testing and counseling. If you are not sure whether you should be tested, call your doctor, the public health department, or the HIV/AIDS hotline listed below. In the meantime, do not participate in activities that put anyone else at risk.

Remember:

➤ HIV infection can be prevented.
➤ HIV is *not* spread through everyday casual contact.

➤ People *cannot* get HIV when they give blood.

National AIDS Information Hotline:

     800-342-AIDS

     800-344-7432 (Spanish)

     800-243-7889 (TTY/TDD)

▼ AFTER AN INJURY OCCURS

RETURN-TO-PLAY GUIDELINES

If an athlete has been injured or ill but seems to have recovered, you may need to decide whether the athlete can safely return to play.

Importance for Athletes

The severity of an injury or illness is not easily determined. An injury or illness that is incorrectly identified and for which the athlete does not receive medical attention may become worse. If medical care is needed, returning to play may be inappropriate after an injury, and sometimes even "sitting it out" through the rest of the practice or competition may be inappropriate. Recovery time may be longer if proper care is delayed, and the athlete could experience increased or permanent damage.

Guidelines for Return to Play

1. Discourage the athlete from returning to play if he or she feels unable to participate.
2. Check the Emergency Reference section of this handbook for actions to take with specific injuries and illnesses. In many cases, the athlete clearly needs medical attention.
3. Know and follow the guidelines for how and when to call 9-1-1 or the local emergency number (p. 51, xiii).

4. The absence of pain does *not* signify the injury is not serious. Do not return an athlete to play simply because he or she says the pain is minimal.
5. With an injury causing pain, swelling, or redness, do not ask the athlete to try to "walk it off." Movement may aggravate the injury.
6. Do not let the athlete move *at all* with any suspected injury to the head, neck, or back. Do not let others touch the athlete or roll him or her over. Call EMS personnel immediately.
7. An athlete with any of the following signals needs immediate medical care:
   ➤ Deformity of limb
   ➤ Any extreme localized pain
   ➤ Joint pain
   ➤ Altered level of consciousness, including drowsiness, disorientation, seizure, unconsciousness
   ➤ Repeated vomiting or diarrhea
   ➤ Unequal pupil size
   ➤ Severe bleeding
   ➤ Breathing difficulty or breathing irregularly
   ➤ Fluid leaking from nose or ears
   ➤ Any eye injury affecting vision
   ➤ Chest pain
8. When in doubt, play it safe and do not let the athlete return to play.
9. Only when none of the above conditions are present is it safe to allow an athlete to return to play. However, never try to advise a reluctant athlete to return. Any athlete who does return to play should be watched closely for any signal that the injury or illness is significant.
10. Following a serious injury or illness, return to play should be guided by a physician's recommendation. These include injuries or illnesses that have resulted in—

- ➤ Unconsciousness.
- ➤ Concussion.
- ➤ Surgery.
- ➤ Missing more than 7 consecutive days of training.

EMERGENCY CARE PERMISSION FORM (SAMPLE)

Athlete's name: _____

Sport: _____

As parent or guardian of the above named athlete, I hereby

authorize the staff of _____

to provide care, including authority for medical transportation,

in the event of injury or illness. I also authorize qualified medical

personnel to provide emergency medical care in the event of an

emergency.

Parent/Guardian: _____

Address: _____

City: _____

State: _____ Zip: _____

Daytime telephone: _____ Evening telephone: _____

Other authorized person to contact in emergency: _____

Relationship to athlete: _____

Daytime telephone: _____

Evening telephone: _____

Family doctor: _____

Doctor's telephone: _____

Athlete's allergies, chronic illnesses, medications taken, or other

medical conditions: _____

Signed: _____

Date: _____

11. The athlete should be able to demonstrate a pain-free full range of motion in the injured areas before returning to play.

REPORTING AND DOCUMENTING INJURIES

All injuries and incidents must be documented and reported appropriately. The facility may already have a form for this purpose, or one can be developed from the following forms.

INSTRUCTIONS FOR EMERGENCY TELEPHONE CALLS

Emergency telephone numbers

(dial ___ for outside line)

EMS: _____

Fire: _____

Police: _____

Poison Control Center: _____

Number of this telephone: _____

Other Important Telephone Numbers

Facility manager: _____

Facility maintenance: _____

Power company: _____

Gas company: _____

Weather bureau: _____

Name and address of medical facility with 24-hour emergency cardiac care: _____

_____

Information for Emergency Call

(Be prepared to give this information to the EMS dispatcher)

1. Location: _____

   Street Address _____

   City or Town _____

   Directions (cross streets, roads, landmarks, etc.): _____

   _____

2. Telephone number from which the call is being made

   _____

3. Caller's name _____

4. What happened _____

5. How many people are injured _____

6. Condition of injured person(s) _____

7. Help (care) being provided _____

Note: Do not hang up first. Let the EMS dispatcher hang up first.

Note: In cities with Enhanced 9-1-1 (911E) systems, it is still important to know the information above for communication to the dispatcher. In many buildings, the telephone system may connect through a switchboard that will show only the corporate address rather than the specific facility from which you are calling. With cellular telephones, 9-1-1E is not functional in identifying a fixed location on the dispatcher's screen. Sharing this information is the only way to provide it.

(Sample Form—post by telephone)

SAMPLE INCIDENT REPORT FORM

Date of report: _____   Date of incident:_____
Time of incident: _____

Facility Information

Facility: _____   Phone #: _____

Address: _____   City _____

State _____   Zip _____

Personal Data - Injured Party

Name: _____ Age: ____ Gender: _____

Address: _____   City _____

State _____   Zip _____

Phone number(s): home: _____

work: _____

Family contact (name and phone #): _____

Incident Data

Location of incident: _____

Description of incident: _____

Was an injury sustained?   Yes ___ No ___

If yes, describe the type of injury sustained: _____

Witnesses _____

1. Name: _____ Phone #: _____

   Address: _____ City _____

   State _____ Zip _____

2. Name: _____ Phone #: _____

   Address: _____ City _____

   State _____ Zip _____

Care Provided

Did victim refuse medical attention by staff?

Yes ___ No ___

Was care provided by facility staff?   Yes ___ No ___

Name of the person who provided care: _____

Describe in detail care provided: _____

_____

Were universal precautions taken?   Yes ___ No ___

Was EMS called? _____

If yes, by whom? _____ Time EMS called: _____

Time EMS arrived: _____

Was the victim transported to an emergency facility? _____

If yes, where? _____

If no, person returned to activity?   Yes___ No ___

If no, what was the referral action taken: _____

_____

Victim's signature (Parent's/Guardian's if victim is a minor):

_____ Date: _____

Facility Data

Number of staff on duty at time of incident: _____

Weather conditions at time of incident: _____

Playing surface conditions at time of incident: _____

Name(s) of staff involved in incident: _____

Report Prepared By:

Name (please print): _____

Position: _____

Signature: _____

TRANSPORTING AN INJURED ATHLETE

Whether you transport an injured athlete or wait for professional medical assistance depends on many factors, including the availability of professional medical assistance, the severity of the injury or illness, and your judgment.

Importance for Athletes

Simple athletic injuries, particularly to the upper extremities, generally are not problematic during transport. Serious injuries of the upper extremities; unstable fractures; head, neck, and back injuries; possible internal injuries; and minor injuries of the lower extremities may require specialized skill when an injured athlete is transported to a medical facility.

Guidelines for Transporting Injured Athletes

1. DO NOT move an athlete with a serious head injury or suspected neck or back injury.
2. If you have doubts about the seriousness of an injury, how to care for an injury, or how to transport an injured athlete, wait for professional medical help.
3. Check the care section of this handbook for actions to take with specific injuries. In many cases, you should call EMS personnel rather than attempt to transport the athlete yourself.
4. Immobilize any musculoskeletal injury before moving an athlete.
5. Allow other athletes to provide assistance to an injured or ill athlete only by following your instructions.
6. Have at least two coaches or athletes accompany the injured athlete when he or she is being transported by anyone other than EMS personnel.

CRITICAL INCIDENT STRESS DEBRIEFING

An emergency involving a serious injury or death is a critical incident. The acute stress it causes for staff, especially the primary rescuer, may overcome a person's ability to cope. This is often called critical incident stress, and it may have a powerful impact. If not appropriately managed, this acute stress may lead to a serious condition called post-traumatic stress syndrome.

Importance to Athletes and Coaches

A person suffering from critical incident stress may become anxious and depressed and be unable to sleep. He or she may have nightmares, nausea, restlessness, loss of appetite, and other problems. Some effects may appear right away and others only after days, weeks, or even months have passed. People suffering from critical incident stress may not be able to perform well in their sport.

Signals of Critical Incident Stress Reactions

➤ Confusion
➤ Lowered attention span
➤ Poor concentration
➤ Denial
➤ Guilt
➤ Depression
➤ Anger
➤ Change in interactions with others
➤ Increased or decreased eating
➤ Uncharacteristic, excessive humor or silence
➤ Unusual behavior

Guidelines to Cope with Critical Incident Stress

This type of stress requires professional help to prevent post-traumatic stress syndrome. Other things the person may do to help reduce stress include using relaxation techniques, eating a balanced diet, avoiding alcohol and drugs, getting enough rest, and participating in some type of physical exercise or activity.

INJURY PREVENTION BIBLIOGRAPHY AND RESOURCE LIST
Publications

Bergeron, J. David, and Holly Wilson Green, *Coaches Guide to Sport Injuries,* 1989, Human Kinetics Books, Champaign, IL.

"Chew or Snuff is Real Bad Stuff," 1993, National Cancer Institute, National Institutes of Health, Public Health Service, U.S. Department of Health and Human Services, Washington, D.C.

"Eating Disorders," 1993, National Institute of Mental Health, National Institutes of Health, Public Health Service, U.S. Department of Health and Human Services, Washington, D.C.

Feigley, David A., editor, *Coaches' Reference Manual, The Rutgers S.A.F.E.T.Y. Clinic,* 1994, Rutgers University, New Brunswick, NJ.

Flegel, Melinda J., *Sport First Aid,* 1992, Leisure Press, Champaign, Illinois.

"Guidelines for Youth Endurance Development," 1991, National Youth Sports Safety Foundation, Inc., Needham, MA.

Heyward, Vivian H., *Advanced Fitness Assessment & Exercise Prescription.*

Howley, Edward T. and B. Don. Franks, *Health Fitness Instructor's Handbook.*

Martens, Rainer, *Successful Coaching,* 1990, Leisure Press, Champaign, IL.

Martens, Rainer, Robert W. Christina, John S. Harvey, Jr., and Brian J. Sharkey, *Coaching Young Athletes,* Human Kinetics Books, Champaign, IL.

Martens, Rainer, and Vern Seefeldt, editors, *Guidelines for Children's Sports,* 1979, American Alliance for Health, Physical Education, Recreation and Dance, Washington D.C.

McArdle, William D., Frank I. Katch, and Victor L. Katch, *Exercise Physiology: Energy, Nutrition, and Human Performance.*

McCann, Sean, and Judy Nelson, "Eating Disorders," *Olympic Coach Vol. 5. No. 1, 1995*

Micheli, Lyle J., *Sportswise: An Essential Guide for Youth Athletes, Parents, and Coaches,* 1990, Houghton Mifflin, Boston.

Overuse Injuries: A Coach's Guide to Understanding Risk Factors, Recognizing Symptoms and Guidelines for Prevention, 1991, National Youth Sports Safety Foundation, Inc., Needham, MA.

"Preparticipation Physical Exams Fact Sheet," National Youth Sports Safety Foundation, Inc., Needham, MA.

Procopio, Deborah, "Doping: Considerations for Coaches," *Olympic Coach,* Vol. 4, No. 4, 1994.

Sports Injury Risk Management & the Keys to Safety, Coalition of Americans to Protect Sports.

"Statistics," National Youth Sports Safety Foundation, Inc., Needham, MA.

"Tips for Athletes," 1991, National Youth Sports Safety Foundation, Inc., Needham, MA.

Wadler, Gary I., "The Coach and Athlete Drug Abuse," *Olympic Coach,* Vol. 6, No. 1, 1996.

"Youth Sports Injuries Fact Sheet," 1994, National Youth Sports Safety Foundation, Inc., Needham, MA.

"Youth Sports Program Guidelines," 1994, National Youth Sports Safety Foundation, Inc., Needham, MA.

Organizations

American College of Sports Medicine
P.O. Box 1440
Indianapolis, IN 46206-1440
(317) 637-9200

American Medical Society for Sports Medicine
7611 Elmwood Avenue, Suite 203
Middleton, WI 53562
(608) 831-4485

American Orthopaedic Society for Sports Medicine
6300 North River Road, Suite 200
Rosemont, IL 60018
(847) 292-4900

American Physical Therapy Association
Sports Physical Therapy Section
505 King Street, Suite 103
LaCrosse, WI 54601
(800) 285-7787

National Association for
Sport and Physical
Education
1900 Association Drive
Reston, VA 22091
(703) 476-3410

National Athletic Trainers'
Association
2952 Stemmons Parkway
Dallas, TX 75247
(214) 637-6282

National Youth Sports Safety
Foundation, Inc.
10 Meredith Circle
Needham, MA 02192-1946
(617) 449-2499

National Governing Bodies

This book provides only general injury prevention information related to many different sports. Sport-specific injury prevention guidelines are just as crucial. Contact the appropriate National Governing Body for additional information related to preventing injury in that sport.

Olympic Division

ARCHERY
National Archery Association
One Olympic Plaza
Colorado Springs, CO 80909
(719) 578-4576

BADMINTON
U.S. Badminton Association
One Olympic Plaza
Colorado Springs, CO 80909
(719) 578-4808

BASEBALL
USA Baseball
2160 Greenwood Ave.
Trenton, NJ 08609
(609) 586-2381

BASKETBALL
USA Basketball
5465 Mark Dabling Blvd.
Colorado Springs, CO
80918-3842
(719) 590-4800

BIATHLON
U.S. Biathlon Association
421 Old Military Rd.
Lake Placid, NY 12946
(518) 523-3836

BOBSLED
U.S. Bobsled and Skeleton
Federation
P.O. Box 828 (421 Old
Military Rd.)
Lake Placid, NY 12946
(518) 523-1842

BOXING
USA Boxing
1520 N. Union Blvd., Suite B
Colorado Springs, CO 80909
(719) 578-4506

CANOE/KAYAK
U.S. Canoe and Kayak Team
Pan American Plaza,
    Suite 610
201 South Capitol Ave.
Indianapolis, IN 46225
(317) 237-5690

American Canoe Association
7432 Alban Station Blvd.,
    Suite B-226
Springfield, VA 22150
(703) 451-0141

CURLING
USA Curling
1100 Center Point Dr.
    (P.O. Box 866)
Stevens Point, WI 54481
(715) 344-1199

CYCLING
USA Cycling, Inc.
One Olympic Plaza
Colorado Springs, CO 80909
(719) 578-4581

DIVING
United States Diving, Inc.
Pan American Plaza,
    Suite 430
201 South Capitol Ave.
Indianapolis, IN 46225
(317) 237-5252

EQUESTRIAN
American Horse Shows
    Association
220 East 42nd St., Suite 409
New York, NY 10017-5876
(212) 972-2472

U.S. Equestrian Team
Pottersville Rd.
Gladstone, NJ 07934
(908) 234-1251

FENCING
U.S. Fencing Association
One Olympic Plaza
Colorado Springs, CO 80909
(719) 578-4511

FIELD HOCKEY
U.S. Field Hockey Association
1520 N. Union Blvd.
Colorado Springs, CO 80909
(719) 578-4567

FIGURE SKATING
U.S. Figure Skating Association
20 First Street
Colorado Springs, CO 80909
(719) 635-5200

GYMNASTICS (Artistic and
    Rhythmic)
USA Gymnastics
Pan American Plaza, Suite 300
201 South Capitol Ave.
Indianapolis, IN 46225
(317) 237-5050

ICE HOCKEY
USA Hockey
4965 North 30th St.
Colorado Springs, CO 80919
(719) 599-5500

JUDO
United States Judo, Inc.
P.O. Box 10013
El Paso, TX 79991
(915) 771-6699

LUGE
U.S. Luge Association
P.O. Box 651 (35 Church St.)
Lake Placid, NY 12946
(518) 523-2071

MODERN PENTATHLON
U.S. Modern Pentathlon
    Association
530 McCullough, Suite 619
San Antonio, TX 78215
(210) 246-3000

ROWING
US Rowing Association
Pan American Plaza,
    Suite 400
201 South Capitol Ave.
Indianapolis, IN 46225
(317) 237-5656

SAILING
United States Sailing
    Association (U.S. Sailing)
P.O. Box 1260 (15 Maritime
    Dr. 02871)
Newport, RI 02871-0924
(401) 683-0800

SHOOTING
USA Shooting
One Olympic Plaza
Colorado Springs, CO 80909
(719) 578-4670

SKIING
U.S. Skiing
P.O. Box 100 (1500
    Kearns Blvd.)
Park City, UT 84060
(801) 649-9090

SOCCER
U.S. Soccer Federation
U.S. Soccer House
1801-1811 South Prairie Ave.
Chicago, IL 60616
(312) 808-1300

SOFTBALL
Amateur Softball Association
2801 N.E. 50th St.
Oklahoma City, OK
    73111-7203
(405) 424-5266

SPEED SKATING
U.S. Speedskating
P.O. Box 16157
Rocky River, OH 44116
(216) 899-0128

SWIMMING
U.S. Swimming, Inc.
One Olympic Plaza
Colorado Springs, CO 80909
(719) 578-4578

SYNCHRONIZED
    SWIMMING
U.S. Synchronized Swimming,
    Inc.
Pan American Plaza, Suite 510
201 South Capitol Ave.
    Indianapolis, IN 46225
    (317) 237-5700

TABLE TENNIS
USA Table Tennis
One Olympic Plaza
Colorado Springs, CO 80909
(719) 578-4583

TEAM HANDBALL
U.S. Team Handball
  Federation
One Olympic Plaza
Colorado Springs, CO 80909
(719) 578-4582

TENNIS
U.S. Tennis Association
70 West Red Oak Ln.
White Plains, NY 10604-3602
(914) 696-7000

TRACK AND FIELD
USA Track and Field
P.O. Box 120 (1 Hoosier
  Dome, Suite 140 46225)
Indianapolis, IN 46206
(317) 261-0500

VOLLEYBALL
USA Volleyball
3595 East Fountain Blvd,
  Suite I-2
Colorado Springs, CO 80910-
  1740
(719) 637-8300

WATER POLO
United States Water Polo
1685 W. Uintah
Colorado Springs, CO 80904
(719) 634-0699

WEIGHTLIFTING
U.S. Weightlifting Federation
One Olympic Plaza
Colorado Springs, CO
  80909-5764
(719) 578-4508

WRESTLING
USA Wrestling
6155 Lehman Dr.
Colorado Springs, CO 80918
(719) 598-8181

Pan American Division

BOWLING
USA Bowling
5301 South 76th St.
Greendale, WI 53129-0500
(414) 421-9008

RACQUETBALL
American Amateur Racquetball
  Association
1685 West Uintah
Colorado Springs, CO 80904
(719) 635-5396

ROLLER SKATING
U.S. Amateur Confederation of
  Roller Skating
P.O. Box 6579 (4730 South St.)
Lincoln, NE 68506
(402) 483-7551

TAEKWONDO
U.S. Taekwondo Union
One Olympic Plaza, Suite 405
Colorado Springs, CO 80909
(719) 578-4632

EMERGENCY REFERENCE

PART TWO

ABDOMINAL INJURY

An abdominal injury may be both open—where organs could be exposed—or closed—with the skin unbroken. Abdominal injuries are serious because there may be significant internal bleeding or damage to organs. The goal is to get help immediately and prevent further injury while waiting for EMS personnel.

SIGNALS OF ABDOMINAL INJURY

➤ Severe pain
➤ Protruding organs
➤ Bruising
➤ Rigid abdominal muscles
➤ Possible external bleeding
➤ Nausea
➤ Vomiting (vomit may include blood)
➤ Weakness
➤ Thirst
➤ Tenderness or a tight feeling in the abdomen

FIRST AID STEPS

CHECK the scene for safety. **CHECK** the injured athlete, following universal precautions when appropriate.
CALL 9-1-1 or the local emergency number.
CARE:

▶ *If organs are exposed in an open wound—*
1. *Do not apply pressure to organs or push them back inside.*
2. Keep the athlete lying down with the knees bent, if that position does not cause pain. Put a folded blanket or pillow under the knees to support them in this position.
3. Remove any clothing from around the wound.

4. Loosely apply moist, sterile dressings or a clean cloth over the wound.
5. Keep the dressing moist with warm water.
6. Place a cloth over the dressing to keep organs warm.
7. Give care to minimize shock (p. 150).

▶ *If organs are not exposed—*

1. Keep the athlete lying down with knees bent, if that position does not cause pain. Put a folded blanket or pillow under the knees to support him or her in this position.
2. Minimize shock (p. 150).

See also Wounds (p. 171).

▲ABDOMINAL PAIN OR DISCOMFORT

Abdominal pain occurring after an injury may be a signal of serious internal injury, even if there is no open wound. Abdominal pain without an obvious cause also may be a signal of a serious injury or illness.

FIRST AID STEPS

CHECK the scene for safety. **CHECK** the injured athlete, following universal precautions when appropriate.
CALL 9-1-1 or the local emergency number if the abdominal pain occurs after an injury or if the athlete has severe abdominal pain that does not go away within 10 to 15 minutes.
CARE:

1. Position the athlete on the back.
2. Allow the athlete to bend the legs slightly if that position is more comfortable.
3. Roll a coat or blanket under the knees.

▶ *If abdominal pain occurs without obvious cause—*

4. Check for other signals.

5. If the athlete has other signals or if the pain is sudden or severe, check for the following problems and give additional care as appropriate:
   ➤ Poisoning (p. 145)
   ➤ Sudden Illness (p. 157)
   ➤ Chest Pain or Pressure (p. 102)
   ➤ Pelvic Injury (p. 142)

See also Abdominal injury (p. 64) for open wounds to the abdomen.

ABDOMINAL THRUSTS *(see Choking, p. 104)*

ABRASION *(see Wounds—Abrasion, p. 172)*

AIRWAY OBSTRUCTION *(see Choking, p. 104)*

ALLERGIC REACTIONS

Allergic reactions to certain food, medication, insect bites and stings, and contact with poisonous plants may cause severe problems, including swelling of the face, eyes, and air passages, which may restrict breathing. The goals are to check for the problem, call for help immediately, and provide care until EMS personnel arrive.

SIGNALS OF ALLERGIC REACTION
➤ Breathing difficulty
➤ Feeling of tightness in the chest and throat
➤ Swelling of the face, neck, and tongue
➤ Rash, hives, or itching
➤ Dizziness or confusion

FIRST AID STEPS
CHECK the scene for safety. **CHECK** the injured athlete for swelling and breathing problems, following uni-

versal precautions when appropriate. Check for a medical alert bracelet.

CALL 9-1-1 or the local emergency number if the athlete has breathing difficulty or shows any of the signs of an allergic reaction.

CARE:
1. Help the athlete into the position most comfortable for breathing.
2. Athletes who know they are allergic may carry a special kit. Assist the athlete as needed with using this kit until help arrives.
3. Be prepared to give additional care for breathing difficulty (p. 89) or other problems that may develop while waiting for EMS personnel.

See also care steps for Poisoning (p. 145).

AMPUTATION *(see Wounds—Amputation, p. 173)*

ANIMAL BITE *(see Bites and stings—Animal bite, p. 74)*

ASTHMA

Asthma is a condition in which air passages become narrow, making breathing difficult. It can be a life-threatening emergency. An attack can be triggered by a reaction to food, medication, insect stings, emotional distress, or physical activity. A young athlete may have exercise-induced asthma without being aware of it.

SIGNALS OF ASTHMA
➤ Breathing difficulty
➤ Wheezing noises
➤ Rapid, shallow breathing, hyperventilation

➤ Tingling or numbness in the fingers or toes
➤ Feelings of fear or confusion

First Aid Steps

CHECK the scene for safety. **CHECK** the injured athlete, following universal precautions when appropriate.
CALL 9-1-1 or the local emergency number if the breathing difficulty does not quickly resolve.
CARE:
1. Help the athlete rest in a position comfortable for breathing.
2. If the athlete has medication for asthma, assist him or her in taking it.
3. Stay with the athlete and watch for signals of breathing difficulty.
4. To minimize shock, keep the athlete from getting chilled or overheated.
5. Calm and reassure the athlete.

See also Breathing difficulty (p. 89).

▼ Back or Neck Injury

Although injuries to the back or neck account for only a small percentage of all injuries, they cause more than half of all injury-related deaths. Signals of a back or neck injury may be sometimes slow to develop and are not always noticeable at first.

Always suspect a back or neck injury in these situations:

➤ A fall from a height greater than the person's height
➤ Any diving mishap
➤ An athlete found unconscious for unknown reasons
➤ Any injury involving severe blunt force to the head or trunk, such as from a boxing punch
➤ Any injury that penetrates the head or trunk, such as a gunshot wound
➤ A motor vehicle crash involving a driver or passengers not wearing safety belts
➤ Any person thrown from a vehicle
➤ Any injury in which an athlete's helmet is broken, including a bicycle, football, or other contact helmet
➤ Any incident involving a lightning strike

SIGNALS OF BACK OR NECK INJURIES

➤ Changes in consciousness
➤ Sudden loss of memory
➤ Loss of balance
➤ Seizures in an athlete who does not have a seizure disorder
➤ Severe pain or pressure in the head, neck, or back
➤ Tingling or loss of sensation in the hands, fingers, feet, or toes
➤ Partial or complete loss of movement of any body part
➤ Unusual bumps or depressions on the head or over the spine
➤ Blood or other fluids draining from the ears or nose
➤ Heavy external bleeding from the head, neck, or back
➤ Impaired breathing or vision as a result of injury
➤ Nausea, vomiting, or persistent headache
➤ Bruising of the head, especially around the eyes and behind the ears

First Aid Steps

CHECK the scene for safety. **CHECK** the injured athlete for consciousness and breathing, following universal precautions when appropriate.

CALL 9-1-1 or the local emergency number.

CARE:

▶ *If the athlete is unconscious—*

1. Keep the athlete's head and neck from moving (see Head injury, p. 123).
2. If the athlete is not breathing, lift the chin without tilting the head back (jaw thrust), pinch the nose shut, and give 2 slow breaths. If air does not go in, carefully tilt the head back to open the airway.
3. Check for a pulse. Give rescue breathing (see Breathing—Stopped, p. 91) or CPR (p. 110), as necessary.
4. Control bleeding (see Bleeding, p. 85).
5. To minimize shock, keep the athlete from getting chilled or overheated.
6. *Do not move the athlete unless absolutely necessary.* If the athlete must be moved, do it carefully without twisting or bending the body. If you are alone, use the athlete's clothes to drag the athlete to safety while supporting the head and neck in the best way possible.

▶ *If the athlete is conscious—*

1. Support the athlete's head in line with the body until EMS personnel arrive.

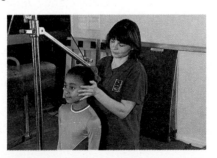

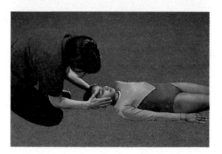

BANDAGING

Bandages are used to hold a dressing in place on a wound and help protect a wound from infection, to maintain pressure on a wound to help control bleeding, to immobilize an injured body part, and to help reduce swelling in certain muscle or joint injuries.

Two commonly used bandages are roller bandages and elastic bandages.

ROLLER BANDAGE

A roller bandage used to control bleeding is called a pressure bandage.

1. Start by securing the bandage over the dressing.

2. Use overlapping turns to cover the dressing completely.

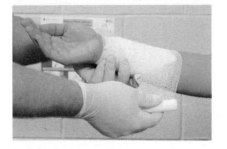

3. Tie or tape the bandage in place.

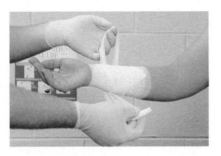

4. Check the fingers for warmth, color, and feeling.

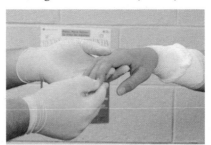

ELASTIC BANDAGE

Elastic bandages control swelling and give support for injuries such as sprains or strains.

1. Start at the point farthest from the heart.

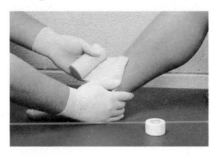

2. Anchor the bandage.

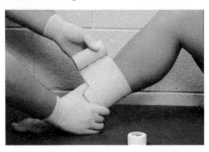

3. Wrap the bandage using overlapping turns.

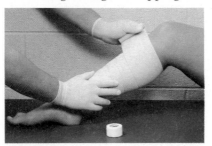

4. Tape the bandage in place.

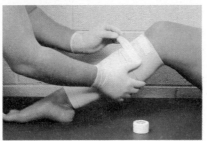

▼ BEE STING *(see Bites and stings—Bee sting, p. 75)*

▼ BITES AND STINGS—ANIMAL BITE

Animal bites can be serious. The goals of care are to control bleeding, get help for possible internal injury, and prevent infection. Remove the animal from the athlete, but do not try to capture it. Report what the animal looked like and the area where it was seen to authorities.

SIGNALS OF ANIMAL BITES
➤ Bite mark
➤ Bleeding
➤ Pain

First Aid Steps

CHECK the scene for safety. **CHECK** the injured athlete, following universal precautions when appropriate.

CALL 9-1-1 or the local emergency number if bleeding is severe or other serious conditions exist.

CARE:

▶ *If bleeding is severe—*

1. Control bleeding (see Bleeding, p. 85).
2. Report the incident to the local animal-control officer or police.

▶ *If bleeding is minor—*

1. Wash the wound with soap and warm water.
2. Control bleeding.
3. Apply antibiotic ointment, spray, or cream.
4. Cover the wound.
5. Report the incident to the local animal-control officer or police.
6. Check with a doctor whether a tetanus booster may be necessary.

▶ *If you suspect that the animal has rabies, get medical attention, regardless of the severity of the injury.*

See also Bleeding (p. 85), Wounds—Puncture (p. 175), and Wounds (p. 171).

▼ Bites and Stings—Bee Sting

A bee sting may be only a painful annoyance or may become a life-threatening emergency for someone who has an allergic reaction. Since you cannot predict whether someone may be allergic, the primary goal of care is to watch for the signals of an allergic reaction and get help immediately.

Signals of Bee Sting

➤ Pain
➤ Swelling

➤ Possible signals of allergic reaction—such as breathing difficulty, swelling, or rash (see Allergic reactions, p. 66 and Breathing difficulty, p. 89)
➤ Stinger stuck in skin

FIRST AID STEPS

CHECK the scene for safety. **CHECK** the injured athlete. **CALL** 9-1-1 or the local emergency number if the athlete shows the signals of an allergic reaction.

CARE:

1. An athlete who knows he or she is allergic to bees may carry a special kit. If needed, help the athlete use it.
2. Remove the stinger with fine-tipped tweezers or by scraping it away with a credit card.
3. Wash the wound with soap and water and bandage it.
4. Apply a cold pack, ice, or other cold item. Place a cloth or towel between the skin and the source of cold.

▼ BITES AND STINGS—HUMAN BITE

A bite from a human may be serious both because of the wound itself and because of the risk of infection. Microorganisms normally carried in the mouth may cause a serious infection if they enter the blood. The goals of care are to call EMS personnel when appropriate, prevent infection, and care for the wound.

SIGNALS OF HUMAN BITE

➤ Bite mark
➤ Bleeding
➤ Pain

FIRST AID STEPS

CHECK the scene for safety. **CHECK** the injured athlete, following universal precautions when appropriate.

CALL 9-1-1 or the local emergency number if the wound bleeds severely or if you suspect the biter may have an infection.

CARE:

▶ *If bleeding is minor—*

1. Wash the wound with soap and warm water.
2. Control bleeding (see Bleeding, p. 85).
3. Apply an antibiotic ointment, cream, or spray.
4. Cover the wound.

▶ *If bleeding is severe—*

1. Control bleeding (see Bleeding, p. 85).

▼ Bites and Stings—Insect Bite

An insect bite may be only a painful annoyance or may become a life-threatening emergency for someone who has an allergic reaction. Since you cannot predict whether someone may be allergic, the primary goal of care is to watch for the signals of an allergic reaction and get help immediately.

SIGNALS OF INSECT BITE

➤ Pain
➤ Swelling
➤ Marks on the skin or a stinger stuck in the skin
➤ Possible signals of an allergic reaction, especially breathing difficulty, swelling, or hives or rash

FIRST AID STEPS

CHECK the scene for safety. **CHECK** the injured athlete, following universal precautions when appropriate.
CALL 9-1-1 or the local emergency number if signals of an allergic reaction develop (p. 66).

CARE:

1. An athlete who knows he or she is allergic to bees may carry a special kit. If needed, help the athlete use it.

2. If there is a stinger in the skin, remove it with tweezers or by scraping it away with a credit card.
3. Wash the wound with soap and water.
4. Cover the wound.
5. Apply a cold pack, ice, or other cold item. Place a cloth or towel between the person's skin and the source of cold.

▼ BITES AND STINGS—JELLYFISH STING

Some types of jellyfish, including the poisonous man-of-war, may sting swimmers and others in the water. If possible, ask local authorities if dangerous jellyfish may be present.

SIGNALS OF JELLYFISH STING
➤ Possible marks on the skin
➤ Pain
➤ Swelling
➤ Possible allergic reaction (p. 66)

FIRST AID STEPS
CHECK the scene for safety. **CHECK** the injured athlete, following universal precautions when appropriate.
CALL 9-1-1 or the local emergency number if—
➤ Breathing difficulty or other signals of allergic reaction develop (p. 66).
➤ The athlete does not know what caused the sting.
➤ The athlete has a history of allergic reactions to marine life stings.
➤ The athlete is stung on the face or neck.
CARE:
1. An athlete who knows he or she is allergic to marine life stings may carry a special kit or medicine. If needed, assist the athlete in using it.

2. Soak the sting area in vinegar, alcohol, or baking soda paste.

BITES AND STINGS—MARINE LIFE STING

Many types of marine life, including some jellyfish, stingrays, some types of coral, spiny urchins, and others, can sting swimmers and others in the water. If possible, ask local authorities what dangerous marine life may be present.

SIGNALS OF MARINE LIFE STING
➤ Possible marks on the skin
➤ Pain
➤ Swelling
➤ Possible signals of allergic reaction, especially breathing difficulty, swelling, or hives or rash

FIRST AID STEPS
CHECK the scene for safety. **CHECK** the injured athlete, following universal precautions when appropriate.
CALL 9-1-1 or the local emergency number if—
➤ Breathing difficulty or other signals of allergic reaction develop, such as swelling, hives, or rash (p. 66).
➤ The athlete does not know what caused the sting.
➤ The athlete has a history of allergic reaction to marine life stings.
➤ The athlete is stung on the face or neck.
CARE:
▶ *If jellyfish sting—*
1. Soak the area in vinegar, alcohol, or baking soda paste.
▶ *If stingray sting—*
1. Immobilize the area.
2. Soak the area in nonscalding hot water until pain goes away.
3. Clean and bandage the wound.

BITES AND STINGS—SCORPION STING

There are several types of scorpions—some poisonous, most not. A scorpion sting may be only a painful annoyance or may become a life-threatening emergency in someone who has an allergic reaction. Since you cannot predict whether someone may be allergic, the primary goal of care is to get help immediately when needed.

SIGNALS OF SCORPION STING

➤ Sting mark
➤ Pain or cramping
➤ Nausea and vomiting
➤ Breathing or swallowing difficulty
➤ Swelling
➤ Rash
➤ Profuse sweating or salivation
➤ Irregular heartbeat

FIRST AID STEPS

CHECK the scene for safety. **CHECK** the injured athlete, following universal precautions when appropriate.
CALL 9-1-1 or the local emergency number; the athlete may need antivenin.
CARE:
1. Watch for the signals of allergic reaction, such as breathing difficulty, swelling, or hives or rash (p. 66).
2. Wash the wound with soap and warm water.
3. Apply a cold pack or other cold object. Place a cloth or towel between the skin and the source of cold.

BITES AND STINGS—SNAKE BITE

The bite of four species of snakes in North America—the rattlesnake, copperhead, water moccasin, and coral snake—is poisonous, and in some cases the bite is life threatening. Do not try to capture the snake, but do note its appearance and provide this information to EMS personnel on arrival.

SIGNALS OF SNAKE BITE
➤ Bite mark
➤ Severe pain and burning
➤ Localized swelling and discoloration

FIRST AID STEPS

CHECK the scene for safety. **CHECK** the injured athlete, following universal precautions when appropriate.

CALL 9-1-1 or the local emergency number unless you are certain the snake is a harmless species and the wound is minor.

CARE:
1. Wash the wound with soap and warm water if possible.
2. Keep the bitten body part still and lower than the heart.
3. Do not apply ice to the wound.
4. Do not cut the wound to try to remove venom.
5. Do not apply a tourniquet.
6. Do not use an electric shock.
7. If possible, carry an athlete who must be moved, or have him or her walk slowly.

Note: If you cannot get professional care within 30 minutes and a snakebite kit is available, consider using the kit to suction the wound.

BITES AND STINGS—SPIDER BITE

The bite of the black widow and brown recluse spiders in North America is poisonous, and in some cases the bite may be life threatening. Do not try to capture the spider, but do note its appearance and provide this information to EMS personnel on arrival.

SIGNALS OF SPIDER BITE
➤ Bite mark
➤ Blistering
➤ Swelling
➤ Profuse sweating or salivation
➤ Irregular heartbeat
➤ Pain or cramping
➤ Nausea and vomiting
➤ Breathing or swallowing difficulty

FIRST AID STEPS
CHECK the scene for safety. **CHECK** the injured athlete, following universal precautions when appropriate.
CALL 9-1-1 or the local emergency number if you are unsure whether the bite was from a spider or other insect or if signals of allergic reaction develop (p. 66).
CARE:
1. Wash the wound with soap and warm water.
2. Apply a cold pack or other cold object. Place a cloth or towel between the skin and the source of cold.

▼ BITES AND STINGS—STINGRAY STING
A stingray sting may be painful and serious for someone who may be allergic. The athlete may not know what form of marine life stung him or her. If possible, ask local authorities what dangerous marine life may be present. The goal of care is to recognize an allergic reaction if one occurs and get emergency medical care for the athlete.

SIGNALS OF STINGRAY STING
➤ Possible marks on skin
➤ Pain
➤ Swelling

➤ Possible signals of allergic reaction, such as breathing difficulty, swelling, or hives or rash

First Aid Steps

CHECK the scene for safety. **CHECK** the injured athlete, following universal precautions when appropriate.
CALL 9-1-1 or the local emergency number if—
➤ The athlete does not know what caused the sting.
➤ The athlete has a history of allergic reactions to marine life stings.
➤ The athlete is stung on the face or neck.
➤ Breathing difficulty or other signals of allergic reaction develop (p. 66).
CARE:
1. Soak the area in nonscalding hot water until pain goes away.
2. Clean and bandage the wound.

▼ Bites and Stings—Tick Bite

A tick bite may transmit Rocky Mountain spotted fever or Lyme disease, which may be serious. The goals of care are to remove the tick from the skin safely and quickly and to watch for developing signals of disease.

Signals of Tick Bite

➤ Tick embedded in the flesh
➤ Sore, reddened area after the tick is removed

Later Signals of Infection from Tick Bite

➤ Fever and chills
➤ Flulike joint and muscle pain
➤ Bull's eye spot or black and blue rash around the bite or on other body parts

First Aid Steps

CHECK the scene for safety. **CHECK** the injured athlete, following universal precautions when appropriate.
CALL 9-1-1 or the local emergency number only if the situation otherwise warrants it.
CARE:

1. Grasp the tick with fine-tipped tweezers close to the skin and pull slowly. Use plastic wrap, paper, or a leaf if you do not have tweezers.

2. *Do not try to burn the tick off.*
3. *Do not apply petroleum jelly or nail polish to the tick.*
4. If you cannot remove the tick or if its mouth parts remain embedded, get medical care.
5. Wash the bite area with soap and warm water.
6. Apply antiseptic or antibiotic ointment.
7. If rash or flulike signals appear, typically within a few days or a few weeks, seek medical attention (see following section).

Ticks and Lyme disease

Not all ticks carry Lyme disease. Lyme disease is spread mainly by the deer tick, a pinhead-size tick found around wooded and grassy areas. Proper clothing and frequent checks for ticks can prevent tick bites. Signals of Lyme disease may develop slowly and might not occur at the same time as the rash. In addition, the rash does not always appear; Lyme disease may still be present.

SIGNALS OF LYME DISEASE
➤ Fever, headache, weakness
➤ Flulike joint and muscle pain
➤ Rash, which starts as a small red area at the site of the bite a few days or a few weeks after the bite:

▶ *On fair skin—*
The center of the rash may be lighter in color, with the outer edges red and raised (bull's eye appearance).

▶ *On dark skin—*
The area may look black and blue.

FIRST AID STEPS
CHECK the scene for safety. **CHECK** the injured athlete, following universal precautions when appropriate.
CALL 9-1-1 or the local emergency number only if the situation otherwise warrants it.
CARE:
1. Make the athlete comfortable.
2. Seek medical attention.
See also Sudden illness (p. 157).

▼BLEEDING

Any serious bleeding may rapidly become life threatening. The goal of care is to control it as quickly as possible in a way that helps protect both the athlete and you from infection.
For *internal bleeding (inside the body), see Internal injury, p. 131.*

First Aid Steps

CHECK the scene for safety. **CHECK** the injured athlete, following universal precautions.

CALL 9-1-1 or the local emergency number for—

➤ Bleeding that cannot be stopped.
➤ Wounds that show muscle or bone.
➤ Wounds that involve joints.
➤ Wounds that gape widely.
➤ Serious wounds that involve hands or feet.
➤ Large or deep wounds.
➤ Large or deeply embedded objects in the wound.
➤ Human or animal bites.
➤ Any wound that would leave an obvious scar, such as on the face.
➤ Skin or body parts that have been partially or completely torn away (see Wounds—Amputation, p. 173).

CARE:

1. Cover the wound with a sterile gauze pad and press firmly. (Only use your bare hand to apply pressure as a last resort.)
2. Elevate the injured area above the level of the heart if you do not suspect broken bones.

3. Cover gauze dressings with a roller bandage to maintain pressure.

▶ *If bleeding does not stop—*
4. If the dressing becomes soaked with blood, *do not remove it*. Apply additional dressings and bandages on top.
5. Squeeze the nearby artery against the bone underneath the artery:

Arm: Inside of the upper arm, between the shoulder and elbow

Leg: Crease at the front of the hip, in the groin

6. Minimize shock, which is likely in an athlete with serious bleeding (p. 150).

See also Bandaging (p. 71) and Wounds (p. 171).

▼ Bone and Joint Injuries

Usually only a trained medical professional can tell the difference between a sprain, strain, fracture, or dislocation. However, you do not need to know what kind of injury it is to provide the appropriate care. A fracture in which the skin is broken by the bone's broken end is an obvious fracture and serious emergency. The primary goal of care is to prevent further injury and get medical attention for the athlete.

SIGNALS OF BONE AND JOINT INJURIES
➤ Pain
➤ Bruising and swelling
➤ Limb deformity
➤ Skin discoloration
➤ Inability to use the affected part normally
➤ Loss of sensation

FIRST AID STEPS
CHECK the scene for safety. **CHECK** the injured athlete, following universal precautions when appropriate.
CALL 9-1-1 or the local emergency number for the following situations:
➤ Limb deformity.
➤ Moderate or severe swelling and discoloration.
➤ Feels or sounds like bones are rubbing together.
➤ "Snap" or "pop" was heard or felt at the time of injury.
➤ A fracture with an open wound on or around the injury site (bone ends may or may not be visible).
➤ Inability to move or use the affected part normally.

➤ The injured area is cold and numb.
➤ The injury involves the head, neck, or back.
➤ The injured athlete has breathing difficulty.
➤ The cause of the injury suggests that the injury may be severe.
➤ Not possible to safely or comfortably move athlete to vehicle for transport to a hospital.

CARE:
1. Avoid any movement or activity that causes pain.
2. Apply ice or a cold pack to control swelling and reduce pain. To prevent further injury, place a towel or cloth between the source of cold and the skin.
3. Splint the arm or leg **only** if the athlete must be moved or transported and if you can do so without causing more pain and discomfort to the athlete (p. 152).
4. To minimize shock, keep the athlete from getting chilled or overheated.

▼BREATHING DIFFICULTY

For breathing that has stopped, see p. 91.

Breathing difficulty may be caused by many types of injury and illness. Common causes follow. Since the problem may worsen and become life threatening, the goals are to check that a problem exists, call EMS personnel when necessary, and care for the specific problem.

SIGNALS OF BREATHING DIFFICULTY
➤ Unusually slow or rapid breathing
➤ Unusually shallow or deep breathing
➤ Gasping for air
➤ Wheezing
➤ Feeling short of breath
➤ Unusually moist or cool skin

- ➤ Flushed, pale, or ashen skin, or bluish appearance
- ➤ Dizziness or lightheadedness
- ➤ Pain in the chest
- ➤ Tingling in the hands and feet

FIRST AID STEPS

CHECK the scene for safety. **CHECK** the injured athlete, following universal precautions when appropriate.
CALL 9-1-1 or the local emergency number if the problem does not resolve itself immediately.
CARE:
1. Check for the possible cause of the problem; ask the athlete about allergies, medications, or conditions.
2. Help the athlete rest in a position comfortable for breathing.
3. Provide enough air: open windows and move bystanders back.
4. Continue to monitor the athlete's condition, and be prepared to give rescue breathing if needed (see Breathing—Stopped, p. 91).

Any of the following may cause breathing difficulty. Look for additional signals of these problems and give the appropriate care:
- ➤ Allergic reaction (p. 66)
- ➤ Asthma (p. 67)
- ➤ Chest injury (p. 101)
- ➤ Chest pain or pressure (p. 102)
- ➤ Choking (p. 104)
- ➤ Drowning (p. 115)
- ➤ Electrical burn (p. 118)
- ➤ Head injury (p. 123)
- ➤ Hyperventilation (p. 128)
- ➤ Poisoning (p. 145)
- ➤ Substance abuse (p. 156)
- ➤ Sudden illness (p. 157)

▼Breathing—Stopped

RESCUE BREATHING

If an athlete's breathing has stopped, regardless of the reason, immediate action is needed to save the athlete's life. Brain cells begin to die within minutes. As soon as you determine breathing has stopped, give rescue breathing.

SIGNALS OF STOPPED BREATHING

➤ Cannot see, feel, or hear breaths
➤ The chest does not rise and fall
➤ The skin appears pale, bluish, or ashen

FIRST AID STEPS

CHECK the scene for safety. **CHECK** the injured athlete, following universal precautions when appropriate.
CALL 9-1-1 or the local emergency number immediately.
CARE:

1. Tilt the athlete's head back and lift the chin. *(Do not tilt a child's head back as far as an adult's.)*

2. Look, listen, and feel for breathing for about 5 seconds.
3. Be alert to special circumstances, such as loose dentures, possible back or neck injury, or neck stoma (see

p. 93 for modifying rescue breathing), or for an object lodged in the throat (see Choking, p. 104).

▶ *If the athlete is not breathing—*

4. Pinch the athlete's nose shut, open your mouth wide, and make a tight seal around the athlete's mouth.
5. Give 2 slow breaths, until the chest gently rises. If the breath does not go in, reposition the head and reattempt breaths. If air still does not go in, the athlete is choking (p. 104).
6. Check for a pulse at the groove beside the windpipe in the neck for about 5 to 10 seconds.

▶ *If the athlete is not breathing and has a pulse—*

7. Give rescue breaths.

Adult: 1 breath
about every 5 seconds

Child: 1 breath
about every 3 seconds

▶ *If the athlete is not breathing and does not have a pulse, start CPR immediately (p. 110).*

8. Recheck pulse and breathing about every minute. Continue rescue breathing as long as a pulse is present but the athlete is not breathing. Check for breathing every few minutes thereafter.
9. If the athlete vomits, carefully turn the athlete on his or her side, wipe the mouth clean, and continue rescue breathing.

▶ *Modify rescue breathing in these circumstances:*

DENTURES/JAW AND MOUTH INJURIES

Dentures that do not remain in place and injuries to the mouth or jaw may make it difficult to make a tight seal around the mouth. Loose dentures may interfere with rescue breathing. If dentures do not remain in place, remove them. A mouth injury may cause the mouth to be tightly shut. Both situations require similar actions.

1. With the athlete's head tilted back, close the mouth by pushing on the chin.
2. Seal your mouth around the athlete's nose.
3. Breathe into the athlete's nose (instead of the mouth) using the same procedure.
4. If possible, open the athlete's mouth between breaths to let air out.

HEAD, NECK, OR BACK INJURY

Head, neck, or back injuries may result from a fall from a height, a violent collision or blow, a diving mishap, or other causes.

1. Attempt to lift the chin without tilting the head back when checking breathing and giving rescue breathing (jaw thrust maneuver).

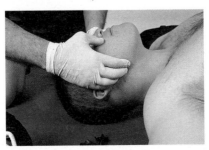

2. If breaths do not go in, tilt the head back only slightly until breaths go in.

3. Remember that the nonbreathing athlete's greatest need is for air.

NECK BREATHING (STOMA)

A person who has had part or all of the voice box removed breathes through a hole in the throat (called a stoma) instead of the mouth and nose. There may be visible scarring at the base of the neck. This person may wear medical alert identification.

1. Check for breathing at the stoma.
2. When giving rescue breaths, breathe into the stoma in the same way you would give breaths at the mouth.

▼ BROKEN BONE *(see Bone and joint injuries, p. 88)*

▼ BRUISE

A bruise is caused by bleeding under the skin resulting from damage to blood vessels or soft tissues. A bruise may signal an internal serious injury.

SIGNALS OF BRUISES

➤ Discoloration (often red first, then purple or dark red)
➤ Pain
➤ Possible swelling

FIRST AID STEPS

CHECK the scene for safety. **CHECK** the injured athlete, following universal precautions when appropriate.
CALL 9-1-1 or the local emergency number if signals of a serious injury are present.

CARE:

▶ *For bruises* not *associated with a serious injury*—

1. Apply ice or a cold pack to help control pain and swelling. To prevent further injury, place a towel or cloth between the ice or cold pack and the skin.
2. Elevate the injured part to reduce swelling.

▶ *If a serious injury may be present*—

3. Check for signals of internal injury (p. 131), bone and joint injuries (p. 88), back or neck injury (p. 68), or head injury (p. 123).
4. Give care for any additional serious conditions found.

See also Muscle injury (p. 137).

BURNS

See also Chemical burn (p. 100) and Electrical burn (p. 118). The care is different in some ways for these kinds of burns.

Burns are caused by heat, chemicals, electricity, and radiation. The severity of a burn depends on the temperature of whatever caused the burn, the length of time the athlete was exposed, the location on the body, the burn's size, and the person's age and medical condition. Burns caused by heat are the most common. The goals of care are to stop the burning, prevent infection, and get medical assistance when needed.

SIGNALS OF BURNS

Superficial burns (see Sunburn, p. 162)

➤ The skin is red and dry.
➤ The area may swell and is usually painful.

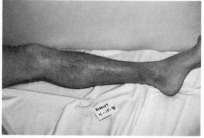

Deep burns
➤ The skin is red and has blisters that may open and ooze clear fluid.
➤ The area may swell and is usually painful.
➤ The area may appear brown or black.
➤ The area may range from relatively painless to extremely painful.

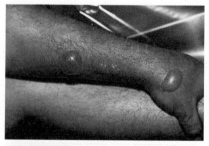

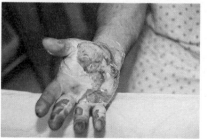

First Aid Steps

CHECK the scene for safety. **CHECK** the injured athlete, following universal precautions when appropriate.

CALL 9-1-1 or the local emergency number for—

➤ Burns involving breathing difficulty.
➤ Burns covering more than one body part.
➤ Burns to the head, neck, hands, feet, or genitals.
➤ Burns (other than very minor) to a child or elderly person.
➤ Burns resulting from chemicals, explosions, or electricity.

CARE:

1. Stop the burning:
   ➤ Remove the athlete from the heat source.
2. Cool the burn:
   ➤ Use large amounts of cool—not icy—water.

➤ Apply soaked towels, sheets, or a wet cloth to the face or other areas that cannot be immersed.
➤ Keep the cloth cool by adding more water.
3. Cover the burn with dry, sterile dressings or a clean cloth.

4. Loosely bandage the dressing in place to prevent infection and reduce pain or cover the burned area with a dry sheet.
5. Keep the athlete comfortable. To minimize shock, keep the athlete from getting chilled or overheated.
6. *DO NOT—*
   ➤ Use ice or ice water except on small surface burns.
   ➤ Put butter or other greasy substances on a burn.
   ➤ Remove any pieces of cloth that stick to a burned area—medical professionals will clean the area.

➤ Break blisters.
➤ Put any kind of ointment on a deep burn or any burn requiring medical attention.

For smoke inhalation, see p. 151.

CARDIAC ARREST *(see Heart—Stopped, p. 126)*

CARDIOPULMONARY RESUSCITATION *(see CPR, p. 110)*

CHARLEY HORSE *(see Muscle injury— Charley horse, p. 138)*

CHECKING AN UNCONSCIOUS ADULT OR CHILD ATHLETE

FIRST AID STEPS

CHECK the scene for safety. **CHECK** the injured athlete, following universal precautions.
CALL 9-1-1 or the local emergency number.
CARE:
1. Tap and shout to see if the athlete responds.
▶ *If the athlete does not respond—*
2. Look, listen, and feel for breathing for 5 seconds.
▶ *If the athlete is not breathing or you cannot tell—*
3. Position the athlete on his or her back while supporting the head and neck.
4. Tilt the head back and lift the chin.

5. Look, listen, and feel for breathing for about 5 seconds.

6. Give 2 slow breaths.

7. Check the pulse for 5 to 10 seconds.

8. Check for severe bleeding.

▼ CHEEK INJURY *(see Mouth injury, p. 133)*

▼ CHEMICAL BURN

A chemical burn may occur anywhere there are chemicals and household substances, including cleansers, field maintenance supplies, or specialized chemicals, such as swimming pool chlorine. Because chemicals continue to burn as long as they are in contact with the skin, the goal of care is first to remove the chemical and then to care for the burn.

SIGNALS OF CHEMICAL BURNS
➤ Presence of substance still on the skin
➤ Skin inflamed, red, or any unusual color
➤ Pain, burning, or stinging sensation

FIRST AID STEPS
CHECK the scene for safety. **CHECK** the injured athlete, following universal precautions when appropriate.
CALL 9-1-1 or the local emergency number.
CARE:
1. Flush both the skin and eyes with large amounts of cool running water until EMS personnel arrive. Always flush away from the body.
2. Remove clothing and jewelry that may trap chemicals against the skin or on which chemicals may have spilled.
3. Keep flushing the affected area until EMS personnel arrive. Be careful not to come in contact with any chemicals yourself.

See also Burns (p. 95).

CHEST INJURY

A chest injury may be an open, bleeding wound or a closed wound with internal injury. A chest wound may be life threatening because of internal or external bleeding, broken bones, injury to internal organs, and breathing difficulty. The goals of first aid are to care for life-threatening conditions and call EMS personnel.

SIGNALS OF CHEST WOUND

➤ Obvious wound or deformity of area
➤ Severe pain
➤ Breathing difficulty
➤ Flushed, pale, ashen, or bluish discoloration of skin
➤ Bruising at the site
➤ Coughing up blood
➤ Sucking noise

FIRST AID STEPS

CHECK the scene for safety. **CHECK** the injured athlete, following universal precautions when appropriate.
CALL 9-1-1 or the local emergency number.
CARE:

1. Keep the athlete from moving and in a comfortable position for breathing.
2. Cover the wound with a sterile dressing or clean cloth and bandage in place.
3. Watch for changes in the athlete's condition.
4. If bubbles are forming around the wound, cover it with plastic wrap or material that does not allow air to pass through. Tape the dressing in place, leaving one corner open to allow air to escape when the athlete exhales.

See also Wounds (p. 171).

▼ CHEST PAIN OR PRESSURE

Chest pain or pressure is the primary signal of a heart attack.

are two general types of cardiac emergency:
heart does not function properly, denying
uscle of much needed oxygen and causing
e., heart attack).
t does not function at all (cardiac arrest)
ped, p. 126).

Anyone can have a heart attack—even a conditioned athlete who seems in excellent health.

Most people who die of heart attacks die within 2 hours after the first signals appear. Many lives are lost because people deny they are having a heart attack and delay calling for help.

Recognizing the signals of a heart attack and then calling EMS personnel before the heart stops are critical steps to saving lives.

Note that a person having a heart attack is likely to deny the possibility of heart attack and call it indigestion or something else.

SIGNALS OF HEART ATTACK

➤ Chest pain or pressure, ranging from discomfort to an unbearable crushing sensation
➤ Pain is not relieved by rest, changing position, or medication
➤ Pain may spread to the shoulder, arm, or jaw
➤ Breathing difficulty
➤ Breathing is often irregular
➤ The person feels short of breath
➤ The pulse may be irregular
➤ The skin may be moist, pale, ashen, or bluish in appearance
➤ The person may sweat profusely

FIRST AID STEPS

CHECK the scene for safety. **CHECK** the injured athlete, following universal precautions when appropriate.
CALL 9-1-1 or the local emergency number immediately.
CARE:
1. Have the person stop activity and rest in a comfortable position. A sitting position may make breathing easier.
2. Loosen restrictive clothing.
3. Assist with prescribed medication.

4. Monitor breathing and pulse closely.
5. Be prepared to give CPR if the person stops breathing and has no pulse (p. 110).

CHOKING

Common causes of choking include trying to swallow large pieces of poorly chewed food; drinking alcohol before and during meals, dulling the nerves that aid in swallowing; eating while talking excitedly or laughing; eating too fast; and walking, playing, or running with food or objects in the mouth. An injured athlete may also choke on dislodged teeth, vomit, or blood.

FIRST AID STEPS

CHECK the scene for safety. **CHECK** the injured athlete, following universal precautions when appropriate.
CALL 9-1-1 or the local emergency number if the athlete continues to cough without clearing the obstruction, cannot speak or cough, or becomes unconscious.
CARE:

▶ *For a choking athlete who can speak or cough—*

1. Encourage the athlete to keep coughing to clear the obstruction.
2. Be prepared to act if the obstruction becomes complete and the athlete cannot breathe (see Choking—Unconscious athlete, p. 106).

▶ *For a choking athlete who CANNOT speak or cough—*

See below for a conscious choking athlete.
See p. 106 for an unconscious choking athlete.

CHOKING—CONSCIOUS ATHLETE

SIGNALS OF A CHOKING CONSCIOUS ATHLETE

➤ Clutching the throat with one or both hands

➤ Unable to speak, cough forcefully, or breathe
➤ High-pitched wheezing

First Aid Steps

CHECK the scene for safety. **CHECK** the injured athlete, following universal precautions when appropriate.
CALL 9-1-1 or the local emergency number.
CARE:
1. Get permission to give care.
2. Perform abdominal thrusts (Heimlich maneuver):
   ➤ Place thumb side of fist against middle of abdomen just above the navel. Grasp fist with other hand.

➤ Give quick, upward thrusts.

3. Repeat until the object is coughed up and the athlete breathes on his or her own or becomes unconscious.
4. If the athlete becomes unconscious, check for an object in the mouth. If the object is visible, sweep it out with a finger **and continue with the choking procedure for an unconscious athlete below.**

CHOKING—UNCONSCIOUS ATHLETE

The airway may become blocked by the tongue falling back in the throat or by food, objects, or fluids, such as blood, saliva, or mucus, becoming lodged in the airway.

SIGNALS OF A CHOKING UNCONSCIOUS ATHLETE

➤ Athlete was observed choking when conscious
➤ Breathing has stopped:
  • Cannot feel or hear breaths
  • The chest does not rise and fall
  • The skin appears pale, bluish, or ashen
➤ Inability to make the chest rise when attempting rescue breaths (p. 91)

FIRST AID STEPS

CHECK the scene for safety. **CHECK** the injured athlete, following universal precautions when appropriate.
CALL 9-1-1 or the local emergency number.
CARE:
1. Position the athlete on the back. Tilt the head back, lift the chin, and pinch the nose shut.
2. Give 2 slow breaths. Breathe in until the chest gently rises.
3. If the athlete's chest does not rise as you attempt to give breaths, retilt the head and try breaths again.

▶ *If air still does not go in—*

    4. Perform abdominal thrusts:

       ➤ Place the heel of one hand on the middle of the abdomen, just above the navel. Place the other hand on top of the first.

       ➤ Give up to 5 quick, upward thrusts.

5. Lift the athlete's lower jaw and tongue and attempt to sweep the object out. (With a child, only attempt to remove object if it is visible.)

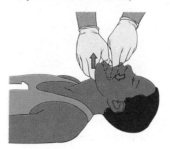

6. Open the airway, tilt the head back, pinch the nose shut, and seal your lips tightly around the person's mouth.
7. Give 2 slow breaths.

▶ *If breaths go in—*

8. Check pulse and breathing.
9. If the athlete has a pulse but is not breathing, do rescue breathing (see Breathing—Stopped, p. 91).
10. If the athlete does not have a pulse and is not breathing, do CPR (p. 110).

▶ *If breaths do not go in—*

8. Continue the sequence beginning with step 3 until you can breathe into the athlete and make the chest rise, the athlete starts to breathe, or EMS personnel arrive.

▼ COLD-RELATED EMERGENCIES

Hypothermia and frostbite are cold-related emergencies. Both conditions may quickly become life or limb threatening. Frostbite is the freezing of body parts (p. 122). Hypothermia is the cooling of the body caused by the failure of the body's warming system (p. 108). The goals of first aid are to restore normal body temperature and to care for any conditions while waiting for EMS personnel.

SIGNALS OF HYPOTHERMIA
➤ Shivering, numbness, glassy stare
➤ Apathy, weakness, impaired judgment
➤ Loss of consciousness

FIRST AID STEPS
CHECK the scene for safety. **CHECK** the injured athlete, following universal precautions when appropriate.
CALL 9-1-1 or the local emergency number.
CARE:
1. Gently move the athlete to a warm place.
2. Monitor breathing and pulse.
3. Give rescue breathing (see Breathing—Stopped, p. 91) and CPR (p. 110) as necessary.
4. Remove any wet clothing and dry the athlete.
5. Warm the athlete *slowly* by wrapping in blankets or by putting dry clothing on the athlete. Hot water bottles and chemical hot packs may be used when first wrapped in a towel or blanket before applying.
6. *Do not warm the athlete too quickly, such as by immersing him or her in warm water.* Rapid warming may cause dangerous heart rhythms.

COMPOUND FRACTURE *(see Bone and joint injuries, p. 88)*

CONCUSSION *(see Head injury, p. 123)*

CONFUSION

Confusion without an obvious cause may be a signal of a serious condition. Check for other signals. If the athlete's confusion is without explanation or is especially severe or if the athlete has other signals, the athlete may have a serious condition. Send someone to call EMS personnel.

While waiting for EMS personnel, look for signals of any of the following conditions that may be possible causes of the confusion, and care for any problem found:

➤ Allergic reactions (p. 66)
➤ Back or neck injury (p. 68)
➤ Chest pain or pressure (p. 102)
➤ Cold-related emergencies (p. 108)
➤ Electrical burn (p. 118)
➤ Head injury (p. 123)
➤ Heat-related emergencies (p. 139)
➤ Hyperventilation (p. 128)
➤ Poisoning (p. 145)
➤ Shock (p. 150)
➤ Substance abuse (p. 156)
➤ Sudden illness—Diabetic emergency (p. 159)
➤ Sudden illness—Stroke (p. 161)

Unless you suspect a specific condition requiring additional care, give the care for sudden illness (p. 157).

◤ CPR

When a heart stops, it causes consciousness to be lost and breathing and pulse to stop. This condition may be caused by heart disease, severe injuries, or electrocution. CPR is given to a person who is not breathing and does not have a pulse. It is a combination of chest compressions and rescue breathing.

▶ *When to perform CPR:*

➤ Not breathing and no pulse

CPR is somewhat different for children (ages 1-8) and adults (ages 9 and up).

For CPR for adults, see below, for CPR for children, see p. 112.

CPR—Adult (Ages 9 and Older)

CPR is performed when the person is unconscious and not breathing and does not have a pulse.

First Aid Steps

CHECK the scene for safety. **CHECK** the injured person, following universal precautions.

CALL 9-1-1 or the local emergency number.

CARE:

1. Check for breathing first.

▶ *If the person is not breathing—*

2. Tilt the head back, pinch the nose, and give 2 slow breaths. Each breath should make the chest gently rise.
3. Check for a pulse at the groove beside the windpipe in the neck.

▶ *If there is a pulse—*

4. Continue rescue breathing as needed.

▶ *If no pulse, begin CPR:*

5. Find your hand position in the center of the chest over the breastbone.

6. Position your shoulders over your hands. Compress the chest to a depth of 1½ to 2 inches 15 times in about 10 seconds.

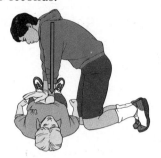

7. Give 2 slow breaths.
8. Do 3 more sets of 15 compressions and 2 breaths.

9. Recheck pulse and breathing for about 5 seconds.
▶ *If there is no pulse, continue sets of 15 compressions and 2 breaths until EMS personnel arrive. Check for breathing and pulse every few minutes thereafter.*

▼ CPR—CHILD (AGES 1 TO 8)

CPR is performed when the child is unconscious and not breathing and does not have a pulse.

FIRST AID STEPS

CHECK the scene for safety. **CHECK** the injured athlete, following universal precautions.

CALL 9-1-1 or the local emergency number.

CARE:

1. Check for breathing.

▶ *If the child is not breathing—*

2. Tilt the head back, pinch the nose, and give 2 slow breaths. Each breath should make the chest gently rise.

3. Check for a pulse at the groove beside the windpipe in the neck.

▶ *If there is a pulse—*

4. Continue rescue breathing as needed.

▶ *If no pulse, begin CPR:*

5. Find your hand position in the center of the chest over the breastbone. Only one hand is used for child CPR.

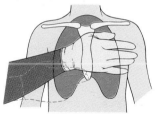

6. Position your shoulder over your hand. Compress the chest to a depth of 1 to $1\frac{1}{2}$ inches 5 times in about 3 seconds.

7. Give 1 slow breath.
8. Repeat cycles of 5 compressions and 1 breath for about 1 minute.

9. Recheck pulse and breathing for about 5 seconds.

▶ *If there is no pulse, continue sets of 5 compressions and 1 breath until EMS personnel arrive. Check pulse and breathing every few minutes thereafter.*

CRAMPS
(see Heat-related emergencies, p. 127 and Muscle injury—cramps, p. 139)

CUTS
(see Bleeding, p. 85 and Wounds, p. 171)

DEHYDRATION
(see Preventing dehydration, p. 30 and Heat-related emergencies, p. 127)

DIABETIC EMERGENCY
(see Sudden illness—Diabetic emergency, p. 159)

DIARRHEA

Ongoing diarrhea may indicate a serious condition. If its onset is sudden and without explanation, look for other signals, consider the following problems as possible causes, and give appropriate care.

➤ Poisoning (p. 145)
➤ Sudden illness (p. 157)

Severe diarrhea may cause a dangerous loss of body

fluid, which may lead to shock and other serious problems (p. 114). Call EMS personnel in severe cases.

DISLOCATION *(see Bone and joint injuries, p. 88)*

In a dislocation, the bone has been displaced from its normal position in a joint. This may be a serious injury. Because only an expert can tell the difference between a fracture and a dislocation, the care given while waiting for EMS personnel is the same (see Bone and joint injuries, p. 88).

DIZZINESS

Feeling dizzy may be a signal of a number of serious conditions, such as the conditions listed below. Look for additional signals that suggest any of these conditions and take the appropriate steps described in these sections:

➤ Allergic reaction (p. 66)
➤ Back or neck injury (p. 68)
➤ Chest pain or pressure (p. 102)
➤ Cold-related emergencies (p. 108)
➤ Electrical burn (p. 118)
➤ Head injury (p. 123)
➤ Heat-related emergencies (p. 139)
➤ Hyperventilation (p. 128)
➤ Poisoning (p. 145)
➤ Shock (p. 150)
➤ Substance abuse (p. 156)
➤ Sudden illness (p. 157)
➤ Sudden illness—Diabetic emergency (p. 159)
➤ Sudden illness—Stroke (p. 161)

See also the care for Fainting (p. 121).

DROWNING

Drowning may happen to anyone in, on, or around the water, regardless of how good a swimmer the athlete is or the nature of the activity. Being able to recognize an athlete who is having trouble in the water may help save the athlete's life. Since the athlete may not be able to call for help, it is important to know the signals of an emergency.

SIGNALS OF NEAR-DROWNING
➤ Struggling movements; little or no forward progress.
➤ The athlete may or may not be able to call or signal for help.
➤ The athlete struggles to breathe.

First Aid Steps
CHECK the scene for safety.
CALL 9-1-1 or the local emergency number.
CARE:
1. Attempt to rescue by reaching or throwing a floating object to the athlete (see Water rescue, p. 168). *Do not attempt a swimming rescue unless trained to do so.*
▶ *Once the athlete is out of the water—*
2. Check the athlete, following universal precautions when appropriate.
3. If the athlete is unconscious, tilt the head back and check for breathing. If not breathing, give 2 slow rescue breaths (see Breathing—Stopped, p. 91).
4. If breaths do not go in, retilt the head and try breaths again.
5. If breaths do not go in, give care for choking (p. 104).
6. Check for a pulse. If no pulse, give CPR (p. 110).
See also Water rescue (p. 168).

▼ DRUGS *(see Substance abuse, p. 156)*

EAR INJURY

Ear injuries include internal injury, such as a rupture of the eardrum from a sudden blow to the head, external injuries, and foreign objects lodged in the ear.

SIGNALS OF EAR INJURY
➤ Blood or fluid draining from the ear
➤ Pain
➤ Loss of hearing

FIRST AID STEPS
CHECK the scene for safety. **CHECK** the injured athlete, following universal precautions when appropriate.
CALL 9-1-1 or the local emergency number if blood or other fluid is draining from the ear or the situation otherwise warrants it.
CARE:
▶ *If there is blood or other fluid draining from the ear—*
1. Cover the ear lightly with a sterile dressing.
▶ *For bleeding around the external ear—*
1. Using a dressing, apply pressure to the wound to control bleeding.
▶ *For suspected internal ear injury—*
1. Seek medical attention.
▶ *For a foreign body lodged in the ear—*
1. If you can see the object, try to grasp and remove it.
2. *Do not try to remove an object with a pin, toothpick, or any sharp item.*
3. Pull down on the earlobe, tilt the head to the side, and shake or gently strike the head on the affected side.
4. If the object does not come out, seek medical assistance.
See also Wounds (p. 171) and Head injury (p. 123).

▼ Electrical Burn

An electrical burn may result from contact with electricity from a power line or cord, equipment, or lightning. **Do not approach an athlete who may still be in contact with electricity.** Often the electrical shock causes problems more serious than the burn that occurs where the skin contacted the electricity, such as breathing or heart problems. Suspect a possible electrical injury if you hear a sudden loud pop or bang or see an unexpected flash of light.

SIGNALS OF ELECTRICAL BURNS
➤ Burn marks on the skin (entry and exit of current)
➤ Unconsciousness
➤ Dazed, confused behavior
➤ Breathing difficulty
➤ Weak, irregular, or absent pulse

First Aid Steps
CHECK the scene for safety. **CHECK** the injured athlete, following universal precautions when appropriate.
CALL 9-1-1 or the local emergency number.
CARE:
1. Never approach an injured athlete in contact with an electrical source until the power is turned off. If a power line is down, wait for the fire department or power company.

2. Check breathing and pulse if the athlete is unconscious. Give rescue breathing (see Breathing—Stopped, p. 91) or CPR (p. 110) if needed.
3. *Do not move the athlete unnecessarily; there may be internal injuries or a back or neck injury.*
4. Check for the possibility of two wounds: entrance and exit burns.
5. *Do not cool the burn area.* (This is different from heat burns.)
6. Cover the burn with a dry, sterile dressing.
7. Take steps to minimize shock (p. 150).

▶ *For a lightning strike—*
1. Look for life-threatening conditions, such as respiratory or cardiac arrest.
2. Check for fractures, including back or neck fracture.
3. *Do not move the athlete.*

See also Burns (p. 95).

ELECTRICAL SHOCK *(see Electrical burn, p. 118)*

EMBEDDED OBJECT *(see Wounds—Embedded object, p. 173)*

EYE INJURY

An eye injury may include injury of tissues around the eye, as well as to the eyeball itself. Injuries that penetrate the eyeball are very serious and may cause blindness.

SIGNALS OF EYE INJURY
➤ Presence of object or substance in eye
➤ Pain, burning sensation
➤ Tears

FIRST AID STEPS
CHECK the scene for safety. **CHECK** the injured athlete, following universal precautions when appropriate.

CALL 9-1-1 or the local emergency number if the situation warrants it.

CARE:
1. *Do not put pressure on the eyeball.*
2. Send someone to call EMS personnel.

▶ *For an object embedded in the eye—*
1. *Do not attempt to remove an object embedded in the eye.*
2. Place a sterile dressing around the object in the eye; stabilize the object, such as with a paper cup, for support.
3. Close and cover the unaffected eye to keep blood, fluid, or dirt from entering it.

▶ *For small foreign bodies in the eye—*
1. Tell the athlete to blink several times to try to remove the object.
2. Gently flush the eye with water.
3. Seek medical attention if the object remains.

▶ *For chemical in the eye—*
1. Flush the eye continuously with water for 10 minutes or until EMS personnel arrive. Always flush away from the uninjured eye.

See also Head injury (p. 123).

Fainting

Fainting is a temporary loss of consciousness. It may be a signal of a more serious condition. The goals of care are to determine if emergency care is needed and care for the athlete until EMS personnel arrive.

First Aid Steps

CHECK the scene for safety. **CHECK** the injured athlete, following universal precautions when appropriate.

CALL 9-1-1 or the local emergency number if you suspect a more serious condition.

CARE:

1. Check breathing and pulse.
2. Elevate the legs 8 to 12 inches if injury is not suspected.
3. Loosen any tight clothing.
4. *Do not give the athlete anything to eat or drink.*

Feeling faint may be a signal of a number of serious conditions, such as the following. Look for additional signals that suggest any of these conditions, and give the care described. If you find no other signals, give care for sudden illness (p. 157).

> ➤ Allergic reactions (p. 66)
> ➤ Back or neck injury (p. 68)
> ➤ Chest pain or pressure (p. 102)
> ➤ Cold-related emergencies (p. 108)
> ➤ Electrical burn (p. 118)
> ➤ Head injury (p. 123)
> ➤ Heat-related emergencies (p. 139)
> ➤ Poisoning (p. 145)
> ➤ Shock (p. 150)
> ➤ Substance abuse (p. 156)
> ➤ Sudden illness—Diabetic emergency (p. 159)

FRACTURE *(see Bone and joint injuries, p. 88)*

FROSTBITE

Frostbite is a cold-related emergency. It may quickly become life or limb threatening. Frostbite is the freezing of a specific body area. (See Cold-related emergencies for care of hypothermia, p. 108.)

SIGNALS OF FROSTBITE

➤ Lack of feeling in the affected area
➤ Skin appears waxy, is cold to the touch, or is discolored (flushed, white or gray, yellow, or blue)

FIRST AID STEPS

CHECK the scene for safety. **CHECK** the injured athlete, following universal precautions when appropriate.
CALL 9-1-1 or the local emergency number.
CARE:

1. Handle the area gently; never rub the affected area.
2. Warm gently by soaking the affected area in warm water (100-105 degrees F) until it appears red and feels warm.

100–105°F ——

3. Loosely bandage the area with dry, sterile dressings.

4. If the athlete's fingers or toes are frostbitten, place dry, sterile gauze between them to keep them separated.
5. Avoid breaking any blisters.

HEADACHE

Headache without an obvious cause may be a signal of a serious condition. Check for other signals. If the athlete's headache is sudden, without explanation, or severe, or if the athlete has other signals, consider the problems listed here and care for the appropriate problem:

➤ Head injury (below) or Back or neck injury (p. 68)
➤ Heat exhaustion or heat stroke (p. 139)
➤ Lyme disease (p. 83)
➤ Poisoning (p. 145)
➤ Sudden illness (p. 157)
➤ Sudden illness—Stroke (p. 161)

HEAD INJURY

Injuries to the head and spine account for more than half of all injury-related deaths. Signals of a head, back, or neck injury may be sometimes slow to develop and are not always noticeable at first. Always consider a possible head, back, or neck injury seriously. A primary goal of care is to prevent further injury caused by movement until EMS personnel arrive.

Always suspect a head injury in these situations:

➤ Significant hard contact with floor boards or objects, especially with the crown or top of the head
➤ A fall from a height greater than the athlete's height
➤ Any diving mishap
➤ An athlete found unconscious for unknown reasons
➤ Any injury involving severe blunt force to the head, such as in football or boxing

- ➤ Any injury that penetrates the head or trunk, such as track shoe spike wounds
- ➤ A motor vehicle crash involving a driver or passengers not wearing safety belts
- ➤ Any person thrown from a motor vehicle
- ➤ Any injury in which an athlete's helmet is broken, including a hockey, football, or cycling helmet
- ➤ Any incident involving a lightning strike

SIGNALS OF HEAD INJURY

- ➤ Changes in consciousness, loss of balance, seizure
- ➤ Severe pain or pressure in the head
- ➤ Tingling or loss of sensation in the hands, fingers, feet, or toes
- ➤ Partial or complete loss of movement of any body part
- ➤ Unusual bumps or depressions on the head
- ➤ Blood or other fluids draining from the ears or nose
- ➤ Heavy external bleeding from the head
- ➤ Impaired breathing or vision as a result of injury
- ➤ Nausea, vomiting, or persistent headache
- ➤ Bruising of the head, especially around the eyes and behind the ears

FIRST AID STEPS

CHECK the scene for safety. **CHECK** the injured athlete, following universal precautions when appropriate.
CALL 9-1-1 or the local emergency number.
CARE:

1. *Do not move the athlete unless absolutely necessary.* If the athlete must be moved, do it carefully without twisting or bending the body. If alone, use the athlete's clothes to drag the athlete to safety while supporting the head and neck in the best way possible.
2. Keep the athlete's head and spine from moving. If you suspect a back or neck injury, support the ath-

lete's head in line with the body until EMS personnel arrive.

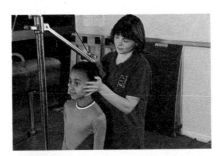

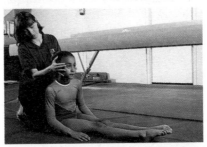

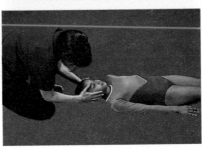

3. Check consciousness and breathing. If the athlete is not breathing, try to lift the chin without tilting the head back (jaw thrust), pinch the nose, and give 2 slow breaths.

4. Check for a pulse. Give rescue breathing or CPR as necessary (see Breathing—Stopped, p. 91 and CPR, p. 110).
5. Control bleeding.
6. To minimize shock, keep the athlete from getting chilled or overheated.

A **concussion** is a temporary impairment of brain function caused by a blow to the head. The primary signals are momentary loss of consciousness and memory loss or confusion. The primary goal of care is to determine whether emergency medical care is needed for a serious condition and to call EMS personnel when appropriate.

▶ *Note: Coaches should be aware that any injury to the head, neck, or back has the potential to be serious or life threatening. If there is any question regarding the extent of the injury, call EMS personnel.*

HEART ATTACK *(see Chest pain or pressure, p. 102)*

HEART—STOPPED *(no pulse)*

When the heart stops, it causes consciousness to be lost and breathing and pulse to stop. This is called cardiac arrest. This condition may be caused by heart disease, severe injuries, or electrocution. CPR is given to a person who is not breathing and does not have a pulse. It is a combination of chest compressions and rescue breathing.

SIGNALS OF STOPPED HEART

➤ Not breathing and no pulse

FIRST AID STEPS

CHECK the scene for safety. **CHECK** the person for consciousness, breathing, and pulse, following universal precautions.

126

CALL 9-1-1 or the local emergency number.
CARE:
1. If no pulse, start CPR immediately (p. 110).
2. If there is a pulse but no breathing, start rescue breathing immediately (see Breathing—Stopped, p. 91).

▼ HEAT CRAMPS *(see Muscle injury—Cramps, p. 139)*

▼ HEAT EXHAUSTION *(see Heat-related emergencies, below)*

▼ HEAT-RELATED EMERGENCIES

Heat-related emergencies are progressive conditions caused by overexposure to heat. If recognized in the early stages, heat-related emergencies can usually be reversed. If not, they may progress to heat stroke, a life-threatening condition.

SIGNALS OF HEAT-RELATED EMERGENCIES

▶ *Early stages (sometimes called heat exhaustion)*
➤ Cool, moist, pale, ashen, or flushed skin
➤ Headache, nausea, dizziness
➤ Weakness, exhaustion
➤ Heavy sweating

▶ *Late stages (sometimes called heat stroke)*
➤ Red, hot, dry skin
➤ Changes in level of consciousness
➤ Vomiting

FIRST AID STEPS

CHECK the scene for safety. **CHECK** the athlete, following universal precautions when appropriate.
CALL 9-1-1 or the local emergency number if the situation warrants.

CARE:

1. Move the athlete to a cool place.
2. Loosen tight clothing.
3. Remove perspiration-soaked clothing.
4. Apply cool, wet cloths to the skin.
5. Fan the athlete.
6. If conscious, give cool water to drink.

▶ *If the athlete refuses water, vomits, or starts to lose consciousness—*

1. Send someone to call EMS personnel.
2. Place the athlete on his or her side.
3. Continue to cool the athlete by using ice or cold packs on the wrists, ankles, groin, and neck and in the armpits.
4. Continue to check breathing and pulse.

See also Muscle injury—Cramps (p. 139).

▼ HEAT STROKE *(see Heat-related emergencies, p. 127)*

▼ HEIMLICH MANEUVER *(see Choking—Conscious athlete, p. 104 or Choking— Unconscious athlete, p. 106)*

▼ HIVES *(see Allergic reactions, p. 66 and Plants— poisonous, p. 144)*

▼ HUMAN BITE *(see Bites and stings—Human bite, p. 76)*

▼ HYPERVENTILATION

Hyperventilation is a breathing problem in which the athlete breathes faster than normal, resulting from fear or anxiety, certain illnesses, or injuries, such as head injuries or severe bleeding. Hyperventilation may be serious because it upsets the body's balance of oxygen and carbon dioxide. It may also be a signal of a more serious problem.

SIGNALS OF HYPERVENTILATION
➤ Rapid, shallow breathing
➤ Feeling of not getting enough air
➤ Fearful, apprehensive feelings
➤ Confusion or dizziness
➤ Tingling or numbness in the fingers and toes

FIRST AID STEPS
CHECK the scene for safety. **CHECK** the athlete, following universal precautions when appropriate.
CALL 9-1-1 or the local emergency number if there are changes in the level of consciousness or breathing difficulty.
CARE:
1. Check for additional signals of serious injury or illness that may be causing the hyperventilation:
   • Asthma (p. 67)
   • Head injury (p. 123)
   • Sudden illness (p. 157)
2. Help the athlete rest in a position comfortable for breathing.
3. Provide enough air: open windows and move bystanders back.
4. Ask the athlete about allergies, medications, or conditions.
5. Send someone to call EMS personnel if the problem does not subside immediately.
6. Continue to monitor the athlete's condition and be prepared to give rescue breathing if needed (see Breathing—Stopped, p. 91).

▼HYPOTHERMIA *(see Cold-related emergencies, p. 108)*

Infection—Preventing

Microorganisms may enter the body through scrapes, cuts, or punctures and cause infection. Infection may develop within hours or days of an injury.

To prevent infection—

▶ *Follow universal precautions (p. 44).*

1. Wash hands before and after caring for the wound, even if you wear gloves.
2. Wash minor wounds with soap and water.
3. *Do not wash wounds that require medical attention unless instructed to do so by a medical professional.*
4. Cover the wound with a clean dressing and bandage; change daily.
5. If infection persists or worsens, have the athlete seek medical help.

SIGNALS OF DEVELOPING INFECTION

➤ The wound area becomes swollen and red.

➤ The area may feel warm or throb with pain.
➤ The area may have a pus discharge.
➤ Red streaks may develop around the wound.
➤ The athlete may develop a fever and feel ill.

Seek medical attention for any developing infection.

INJURY, SEE SPECIFIC BODY AREAS INJURED

INSECT BITE *(see Bites and stings—Insect bite, p. 77)*

INTERNAL INJURY

Internal injuries include internal bleeding and injury to organs. Such injuries may result from blunt blows to the body. Internal injury may be more difficult to recognize because the signals may develop more gradually, yet these injuries may be life threatening. The goals of first aid are to recognize when there may be an internal injury and provide care while waiting for EMS personnel to arrive.

SIGNALS OF INTERNAL INJURY

➤ Bruising in area
➤ Tender, swollen, or hard area (such as abdomen)
➤ Anxiety or restlessness
➤ Rapid, weak pulse
➤ Rapid breathing
➤ Skin that feels cool or moist or looks pale, bluish, or ashen

➤ Nausea or vomiting
➤ Excessive thirst
➤ Declining level of consciousness

FIRST AID STEPS

CHECK the scene for safety. **CHECK** the injured athlete, following universal precautions when appropriate.
CALL 9-1-1 or the local emergency number if the situation warrants it.
CARE:
1. Help the athlete rest in the most comfortable position.
2. To minimize shock, keep the athlete from getting chilled or overheated (p. 150).
3. Reassure the athlete.
See also Abdominal injury (p. 64), Chest injury (p. 101), Pelvic injury (p. 142), and Head injury (p. 123)

ITCHING *(see Allergic reactions, p. 66 and Plants— Poisonous, p. 144)*

JELLYFISH STING *(see Bites and stings—Jellyfish sting, p. 78)*

JOINT INJURY *(see Bone and joint injuries, p. 88)*

LIGHTNING STRIKE *(see Electrical burn, p. 118)*

LOSS OF SENSATION

A loss of sensation (paralysis) usually signals a serious injury to the head or neck or other body area.

SIGNALS OF LOSS OF SENSATION

➤ The athlete is unable to move his or her legs or body below a certain point.
➤ Tingling or numbness in the fingers or toes.

FIRST AID STEPS

CHECK the scene for safety. **CHECK** the injured athlete, following universal precautions when appropriate.
CALL 9-1-1 or the local emergency number.
CARE as for a back or neck injury:

1. Keep the athlete from moving, and immobilize the head and neck.
2. Check consciousness and breathing. If the athlete is not breathing, try to lift the chin without tilting the head back, pinch the nose, and give 2 slow breaths.
3. Check for a pulse. Give rescue breathing (see Breathing—Stopped, p. 91) or CPR (p. 110), as necessary.
4. Control any bleeding.
5. To minimize shock, keep the athlete from getting chilled or overheated.
6. *Do not move the athlete unless absolutely necessary.* If the athlete must be moved, do it carefully without twisting or bending the body. If alone, use the athlete's clothes to drag the athlete to safety while supporting the head and neck in the best way possible.

See also Cold-related emergencies (p. 108), Back or neck injury (p. 68), Head injury (p. 123), Bone and joint injuries (p. 88), and Sudden illness (p. 157).

▼LYME DISEASE *(see Bites and stings—Tick bite, p. 83)*

▼MARINE LIFE STING *(see Bites and stings—Marine life sting, p. 79)*

▼MOUTH INJURY

A mouth injury may occur inside or outside the mouth. Bleeding may be heavy. As with any wound, the priority is to control bleeding with a sterile dressing and apply pressure on the wound.

First Aid Steps

CHECK the scene for safety. **CHECK** the injured athlete, following universal precautions when appropriate.

CALL 9-1-1 or the local emergency number if there are signals of a head, neck, or back injury, changes in level of consciousness, or breathing difficulty.

CARE:

▶ *If no serious head, back, or neck injury is suspected—*

1. Have the athlete lean slightly forward or place the athlete on his or her side.
2. Try to prevent the athlete from swallowing the blood, which may cause nausea or vomiting.
3. Apply the dressing:
   ▶ *For inside the cheek—*
      ➤ Place folded sterile dressings inside the mouth against the wound.
   ▶ *For outside the cheek—*
      ➤ Apply direct pressure using a sterile dressing.
   ▶ *For the tongue or lips—*
      ➤ Apply direct pressure using a sterile dressing.
      ➤ Apply cold to reduce swelling and ease pain.
4. If teeth have been knocked out, see also Teeth— Knocked out (p. 164).

▶ *If the injury to the mouth or cheek may be associated with a more serious head, neck, or back injury—*

1. Care for a head injury (p. 123) or back or neck injury (p. 68).

See also Wounds (p. 171).

▼ Moving an Injured Athlete

Moving an athlete may make some injuries worse. **You should move an athlete only if there is immediate danger or the athlete has to be moved to give proper care.** Even if you are in a remote area, such as when camping, it is often easier to bring professional medical help to the injured or ill athlete than the athlete to the help. Once you decide to move someone, you must determine how to move them. Always consider your safety and the safety of the athlete.

Clothes drag—used for an athlete with suspected head, neck, or back injury.

Walking assist—used for a conscious athlete without suspected serious injury.

Two-person seat carry—used for an athlete without suspected head, neck, or back injury.

MUSCLE CRAMPS *(see Muscle injury—Cramps, p. 139)*

MUSCLE INJURY

Usually only a trained medical professional can tell the difference between a muscle injury, such as a strain, and a bone or joint injury, such as a fracture or dislocation. However, you do not need to know what kind of injury it is to provide the correct care. The primary goal of care is to prevent further injury and get medical attention for the athlete.

SIGNALS OF MUSCLE INJURIES
➤ Pain
➤ Bruising and swelling

FIRST AID STEPS
CHECK the scene for safety. **CHECK** the injured athlete, following universal precautions when appropriate.
CALL 9-1-1 or the local emergency number for the following situations:
➤ Limb deformity
➤ Feels or sounds like bones are rubbing together
➤ "Snap" or "pop" was heard or felt at the time of injury
➤ Inability to move or use the affected part normally
➤ The injured area is cold and numb
➤ The injury involves the head, neck, or back
➤ The injured athlete has breathing difficulty
➤ The cause of the injury suggests that it may be severe
➤ Not possible to safely or comfortably move the athlete to a vehicle for transport to a hospital

CARE:
1. Avoid moving the injured part.
2. Apply ice or a cold pack to control swelling and reduce pain. To prevent further injury, place a towel or cloth between the source of cold and the skin.
3. Avoid any movement or activity that causes pain.

▶ *If you suspect a serious injury—*
  4. Keep the athlete still and the injured part from moving.

Splint the arm or leg only if the athlete must be moved or transported and if you can do so without causing more pain and discomfort to the athlete (p. 152).

See also Muscle injury—Charley horse (p. 138), Muscle injury—Cramps (p. 139), and Muscle Injury—Pulled Muscle (p. 140).

▽ MUSCLE INJURY—CHARLEY HORSE

A direct blow or muscle overuse may result in a painful condition known as a charley horse, a type of muscle strain or bruise.

SIGNALS OF CHARLEY HORSE
➤ Localized pain
➤ Swelling
➤ Loss of motion in the muscle

FIRST AID STEPS
CHECK the scene for safety. **CHECK** the injured athlete, following universal precautions when appropriate.
CALL 9-1-1 or the local emergency number if there are signals of a serious injury.
CARE:
1. Care for any more serious injuries suspected, such as bone or joint injury (p. 88).
▶ *For a charley horse (in the absence of a more serious injury)—*
  2. Apply ice 20 minutes on, 20 minutes off.
  3. Apply an elastic bandage above, over, and below the area, without leaving an opening for swelling to develop or blood to pool.

138

4. Stretch slowly while icing.
5. *Do not apply heat.*
6. *Do not bounce on the affected leg.*
7. *Do not continue athletic activity while signals persist.*
See also Muscle injury (p. 137).

MUSCLE INJURY—CRAMPS

A muscle cramp is a sudden muscle contraction resulting from overuse or cold, usually occurring in the arm, foot, or calf. Such an injury is serious only if it puts the athlete in a life-threatening situation, such as a swimmer who is unable to reach safety after a cramp occurs. A cramp of abdominal muscles may be mistakenly called a stomach cramp. A heat cramp is a muscle cramp that results from overheating.

SIGNALS OF MUSCLE CRAMPS
➤ Immediate tightness and spasm in the muscle
➤ Pain

FIRST AID STEPS
CHECK the scene for safety. Check the injured athlete, following universal precautions when appropriate.
CALL 9-1-1 or the local emergency number if there are any signals of a serious condition.
CARE:
1. Have the athlete stop activity; a swimmer should leave the water.
2. Stretch the affected area immediately; for a leg cramp, extend the leg and flex the ankle.
3. Massage the area of muscle where the spasm is occurring.
4. For an abdominal cramp, help the athlete get comfortable and rest. Ensure the cramp was caused by

exertion or cold water, not by a possible internal injury (p. 131) or sudden illness (p. 157).

5. For muscle cramps related to being overheated, have the athlete rest in a cool place and give cool water or a commercial sports drink. Watch for the signals of heat-related emergencies (p. 139) and send someone to call EMS personnel if necessary.

See also Muscle injury (p. 137) and Bone and joint injuries (p. 88).

▼ Muscle Injury—Pulled Muscle

A pulled muscle is a type of muscle strain, which is a stretching and tearing of muscles or tendons. It may result from improper stretching, muscular overuse, or a sudden twisting motion.

Signals of Pulled Muscle
➤ Pain
➤ Tightness in muscle
➤ Swelling
➤ Occasional loss of motion if severe

First Aid Steps
CHECK the scene for safety. **CHECK** the injured athlete, following universal precautions when appropriate.
CALL 9-1-1 or the local emergency number if there are any signals of a serious condition.
CARE:
1. Apply ice 20 minutes on, 20 minutes off.
2. Wrap the area with an elastic bandage.
3. Seek medical advice before resuming athletic activities.

Be careful not to assume a possibly serious injury is only a pulled muscle. Any injury involving bones or joints may be more serious.

See also Bone and joint injuries (p. 88).

NAUSEA

Nausea without an obvious cause may be a signal of a serious condition. Check for other signals. If the athlete's nausea is without explanation or is especially severe or if the athlete has other signals, the goals of first aid are to check the athlete for the problems listed here and care for any problem found.

➤ Head injury (p. 123) or Back or neck injury (p. 68)
➤ Heat-related emergencies (p. 139)
➤ Internal injury (p. 131)
➤ Poisoning (p. 145)
➤ Sudden illness (p. 157)

FIRST AID STEPS

CHECK the scene for safety. **CHECK** the athlete, following universal precautions when appropriate.
CALL 9-1-1 or the local emergency number if there are signals of a serious condition.
CARE:
1. Be prepared to give care for vomiting (p. 167).
2. Care for specific problems found, and care for sudden illness (p. 157).

NECK INJURY *(see Back or neck injury, p. 68)*

NOSEBLEED

Nosebleeds are typically caused by a blunt blow to the nose. Bleeding may be heavy at first.

FIRST AID STEPS

CHECK the scene for safety. **CHECK** the injured athlete, following universal precautions when appropriate.
CALL 9-1-1 or the local emergency number if you suspect a head, neck, or back injury or other serious condition.

CARE:
1. Have the athlete sit leaning slightly forward.
2. Pinch the nostrils together for about 10 minutes.
3. Apply an ice pack to the bridge of the nose.

▶ *If bleeding does not stop—*

4. Apply pressure on the upper lip just beneath the nose.
5. Seek medical attention if the bleeding persists or recurs or if the athlete says it is the result of high blood pressure.
6. Send someone to call EMS personnel if the athlete loses consciousness; position the athlete on the side to allow blood to drain from the nose.

▶ *After the bleeding stops—*

7. Have the athlete avoid rubbing, blowing, or picking the nose, which could restart the bleeding.
8. Later, you may apply petroleum jelly inside the nostril to help keep it moist.

If the injury to the mouth or cheek may be associated with a more serious head, neck, or back injury, see Head injury (p. 123) or Back or neck injury (p. 68).

▼PARALYSIS *(see Loss of sensation, p. 132)*

▼PELVIC INJURY

An injury to the pelvis may be serious or life threatening because of the risk of damage to major arteries or internal organs. Fracture of bones in this area may cause severe internal bleeding. The goals of first aid are to check for a potential serious injury, obtain immediate emergency medical care, and care for the athlete until EMS personnel arrive.

SIGNALS OF PELVIC INJURY
➤ Severe pain
➤ Bruising

➤ Possible external bleeding
➤ Nausea
➤ Vomiting (vomit may include blood)
➤ Weakness
➤ Thirst
➤ Tenderness or a tight feeling in the abdomen
➤ Possible loss of sensation in the legs or inability to move the legs

FIRST AID STEPS

CHECK the scene for safety. **CHECK** the injured athlete, following universal precautions when appropriate.
CALL 9-1-1 or the local emergency number.
CARE:
1. Do not move the athlete because of the possibility of a back or neck injury.

▶ *If organs are exposed in an open wound—*
2. Keep the athlete lying flat if that position does not cause pain; otherwise keep the athlete in a comfortable position.
3. Remove any clothing from around the wound.
4. *Do not apply pressure to organs or push them back inside.*
5. Apply moist, sterile dressings or a clean cloth loosely over the wound.
6. Keep the dressing moist with warm water.
7. Place a cloth over the dressing to keep organs warm.
8. Give care to minimize shock (p. 150).

▶ *If organs are not exposed—*
2. Keep the athlete lying flat if that position does not cause pain; otherwise keep the athlete in a comfortable position.
3. Give care to minimize shock (p. 150).
For care for possible back or neck injury, see p. 68.

PLANTS—POISONOUS

Poison ivy, poison oak, and poison sumac are the most common poisonous plants. Some people are allergic to these plants and have dramatic reactions after contact, while others may not even have a rash.

A, Poison ivy

B, Poison sumac

C, Poison oak

SIGNALS OF CONTACT WITH POISONOUS PLANTS

➤ Itching
➤ Red rash, often progressing to weeping sores
➤ Swelling

FIRST AID STEPS

CHECK the scene for safety. **CHECK** the athlete, following universal precautions when appropriate.

CALL 9-1-1 or the local emergency number if there are signals of a serious condition.

CARE:

1. Immediately wash the affected area thoroughly with soap and water.
2. If a rash or open sores develop, apply a paste of baking soda and water several times a day to reduce discomfort.
3. Lotions, such as calamine or Caladryl®, may help soothe the area. Antihistamines, such as Benadryl®, may also help dry up the sores.
4. If the condition worsens or affects large areas of the body or face, seek medical attention.

▼
POISON IVY, POISON OAK, ETC. *(see Plants— Poisonous, p. 144)*

▼
POISONING

A poison is a substance that causes injury or illness if it enters the body. There are four ways a poison may enter the body—by swallowing it, breathing it, touching it, or having it injected. Combinations of certain substances, such as drugs and alcohol, may be poisonous, although if taken by themselves they might not cause harm. Not everyone reacts to poisons in the same way. A substance that is harmful to one may not always be harmful to another.

Many poisonings can be cared for without the help of EMS personnel. Poison Control Center (PCC) personnel have access to information on most poisonous substances and can tell you what care to give to counteract the poison.

Keep your PCC telephone number posted by the telephone. Also record it on the inside back cover of this guide. You can find the number of your PCC in the inside front cover of the phone book.

SIGNALS OF POISONING

➤ Breathing difficulty
➤ Nausea, vomiting, diarrhea
➤ Chest or abdominal pain
➤ Sweating, changes in consciousness, seizure
➤ Headache
➤ Dizziness
➤ Irregular pupil size
➤ Burning/tearing of the eyes
➤ Abnormal skin color
➤ Burns around the lips, tongue, or on the skin
➤ Open or spilled containers
➤ Unusual odors, flames, smoke
➤ Unusual behavior suggesting drug use

Allergic reactions are also a type of poisoning and may be life threatening (p. 66).

FIRST AID STEPS

CHECK the scene to make sure it is safe to approach.
CHECK the athlete, following universal precautions when appropriate.

➤ Gather clues about what happened.
➤ Look for any containers and have the caller take them to the telephone.
➤ If you suspect someone has swallowed a poison, try to find out what type of poison it was, how much was taken, and when it was taken.

146

CALL 9-1-1 or the local emergency number or the PCC as appropriate.

CARE:

1. If necessary, move the athlete to safety, away from the source of the poison.
2. Check the athlete's level of consciousness, breathing, and pulse.
3. Care for any life-threatening conditions first.
4. *Never give anything to eat or drink unless directed to do so by the PCC or a medical professional.*
5. If the athlete vomits, position the athlete on his or her side. Save a sample of the vomit if the poison is not known so that the poison can be identified if necessary.

Note: In cases of poisoning by a substance in contact with the skin, wash the area thoroughly with running water (see Chemical burn, p. 100).

PULLED MUSCLE *(see Muscle injury—Pulled muscle, p. 140)*

PUNCTURE WOUND *(see Wounds—Puncture, p. 175)*

RASH *(see Allergic reactions, p. 66 and Plants—Poisonous, p. 144)*

RESCUE BREATHING *(see Breathing—Stopped, p. 91)*

SCALP INJURY

Scalp bleeding may be minor or severe. Although bleeding is usually easily controlled with pressure, be careful in case the skull may be fractured. The goals of care are to recognize a serious injury, get emergency help, and control bleeding.

SIGNALS OF SCALP INJURY
➤ Bleeding
➤ Open wound

▶ *Signals of skull fracture*
➤ Depression in the skull
➤ Spongy feeling of the scalp
➤ Bone fragments in the wound

FIRST AID STEPS
CHECK the scene for safety. **CHECK** the injured athlete, following universal precautions when appropriate.
CALL 9-1-1 or the local emergency number if there are signals of a serious condition.
CARE:
1. Apply gentle pressure around the wound over a dressing; feel for the signals of a possible skull fracture.

▶ *If there is a risk of a skull fracture—*
2. Call 9-1-1 or the local emergency number if you have not already.
3. *DO NOT put pressure directly on the wound.*
4. Try to control bleeding with pressure on the area *around* the wound.

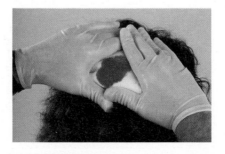

▶ *If there is no risk of a skull fracture—*

2. Control the bleeding with direct pressure on the dressings.

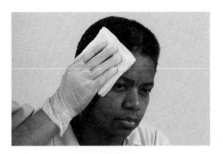

3. Secure dressings in place with a roller bandage.

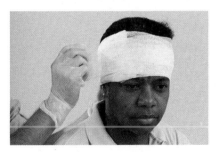

If the scalp injury is associated with a more serious head, neck, or back injury, see Head injury (p. 123) or Back or neck injury (p. 68).

See also Head injury, p. 123.

SCORPION STING *(see Bites and stings—Scorpion sting, p. 80)*

SCRAPES *(see Wounds—Abrasion, p. 172)*

SEIZURE *(see Sudden illness—Seizure, p. 160)*

SEVERED BODY PART *(see Wounds—Amputation, p. 173)*

SHOCK

Shock is a life-threatening condition in which not enough blood is being delivered to all parts of the body. Body organs begin to fail. Shock may be caused by severe bleeding, serious internal injury, significant fluid loss, or other conditions. An athlete going into shock needs immediate medical attention. The goals of first aid are to obtain help quickly and give care to minimize shock while caring for the injury or illness.

SIGNALS OF SHOCK
➤ Restlessness or irritability
➤ Altered consciousness
➤ Pale or ashen, cool, moist skin
➤ Rapid breathing
➤ Rapid pulse
➤ Excessive thirst
➤ Nausea or vomiting

FIRST AID STEPS
CHECK the scene for safety. **CHECK** the injured athlete, following universal precautions when appropriate.
CALL 9-1-1 or the local emergency number.
CARE:
1. Have the athlete lie down and rest comfortably (pain worsens shock).
2. Control any external bleeding (see Bleeding, p. 85).
3. Keep the athlete from getting chilled or overheated.
4. Reassure the athlete (anxiety may worsen shock).

5. Unless you suspect a head, neck, or back injury or broken bones in the hips or legs, elevate the legs about 12 inches.
6. Do not give anything to drink or eat, even though the athlete may ask for it.

See also Bleeding (p. 85), Internal injury (p. 131), and Fainting (p. 121).

SMOKE INHALATION

Smoke inhalation may injure respiratory passages or the lungs, affecting breathing and the oxygenation of blood. It may be life threatening.

SIGNALS OF SMOKE INHALATION
➤ Breathing difficulty
➤ Coughing
➤ Burns, ash, or soot about the nose or mouth

FIRST AID STEPS
CHECK the scene for safety. **CHECK** the injured athlete, following universal precautions when appropriate.
CALL 9-1-1 or the local emergency number.
CARE:
1. Move the athlete to fresh air.
2. Check breathing and pulse.

▶ *If the athlete is conscious—*

3. Support the athlete in the position in which it is easiest to breathe and monitor breathing.

▶ *If the athlete is unconscious—*

3. Place the athlete on his or her side and monitor breathing closely.

See also Burns (p. 95) and Breathing difficulty (p. 89).

SNAKE BITE *(see Bites and stings—Snake bite, p. 80)*

SPIDER BITE *(see Bites and stings—Spider bite, p. 81)*

SPINAL INJURY *(see Back or neck injury, p. 68)*

SPLINTING *(immobilization)*

Splinting is a method of immobilizing an injured body part to keep it from moving. It may also help to reduce pain, making the injured athlete more comfortable. **Splint only if the athlete must be moved or transported and if you can do so without causing more pain and discomfort to the athlete.** Immobilization may be used when appropriate for any musculoskeletal injury, including fractures, dislocations, sprains, and joint injuries. You do not need to know the specific type of injury before deciding to splint it.

IMMOBILIZATION GUIDELINES

➤ Immobilize an injury in the position you find it.
➤ Immobilize the joints above and below an injured bone.
➤ Immobilize the bones above and below an injured joint.
➤ Check for warmth and color of the skin below the site of the injury both before and after splinting.

METHODS

There are a variety of ways to immobilize an injured body part. Choose a method using materials at hand that will best keep the injured part from moving. Simply supporting the injured part in the position you find it, such as placing a small pillow or folded blanket under an injured leg against the ground, is the best method of all.

ANATOMIC SPLINT

A part of the body used to immobilize the injured part (an injured leg can be splinted to an uninjured leg).

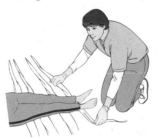

SOFT SPLINT

Made with soft materials, such as folded blankets, towels, or pillows.

SLING

A triangular bandage tied to support an injured arm, wrist, or hand.

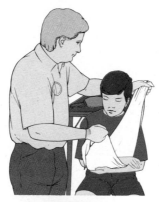

RIGID SPLINT

Made with boards, folded magazines, newspaper, or metal strips.

See also Bone and joint injuries (p. 88).

▼**S**PRAINS *(see Bone and joint injuries, p. 88)*

▼**S**TINGRAY **S**TING *(see Bites and stings—Stingray sting, p. 82)*

▼**S**TINGS *(see Bites and stings, pp. 74–85)*

▼**S**TRAINS *(see Muscle injury, p. 137)*

STROKE *(see Sudden illness—Stroke, p. 161)*

SUBSTANCE ABUSE

A wide range of drugs and other substances are abused in our society, with a wide range of psychological and physical effects. Your goal is not to try to diagnose a clear case of the athlete being under the influence of a drug or other substance. The goal of care is to recognize a possible overdose or other problem requiring medical attention or other professional help. Do not be judgmental or assume an illegal drug is involved. Instead, treat the situation like any other case of sudden illness (p. 157).

SIGNALS OF SUBSTANCE ABUSE

➤ Behavioral changes not otherwise explained
➤ Sudden mood changes
➤ Restlessness, talkativeness, irritability
➤ Altered consciousness
➤ Slurred speech, poor coordination
➤ Moist or flushed skin
➤ Chills, nausea, vomiting
➤ Dizziness, confusion
➤ Irregular pulse
➤ Irregular breathing
➤ Loss of consciousness

FIRST AID STEPS

CHECK the scene for safety. **CHECK** the injured athlete, following universal precautions when appropriate.
CALL the local Poison Control Center and follow their directions if you have good reason to suspect a substance was taken. **CALL** 9-1-1 or the local emergency number if—
➤ The athlete is unconscious, confused, or seems to be losing consciousness.

- ➤ The athlete has breathing difficulty or is breathing irregularly.
- ➤ The athlete has persistent chest pain or pressure.
- ➤ The athlete has pressure or pain in the abdomen that does not go away.
- ➤ The athlete is vomiting or passing blood.
- ➤ The athlete has a seizure, severe headache, or slurred speech.
- ➤ The athlete engages in violent behavior.
- ➤ You are unsure what to do.
- ➤ You are unsure about the severity of the problem.

CARE:

1. Try to learn from others what substance may have been taken.
2. Calm and reassure the athlete.
3. To minimize shock, keep the athlete from getting chilled or overheated.

See also Poisoning (p. 145) and Sudden illness (below).

▼ Sudden Illness

Many different types of sudden illness often have similar signals. Usually you will not know the exact cause of the illness, but this should not keep you from providing care. Care for the signals you find.

SIGNALS OF SUDDEN ILLNESS

- ➤ Feeling lightheaded, dizzy, confused, or weak
- ➤ Changes in skin color (pale, ashen, or flushed skin), sweating
- ➤ Nausea, vomiting, or diarrhea

Some illnesses may also include the following:

- ➤ Seizure or changes in consciousness

➤ Paralysis (inability to move), slurred speech, or blurred vision
➤ Severe headache, breathing difficulty, persistent pressure or pain

FIRST AID STEPS

CHECK the scene for safety. **CHECK** the injured athlete, following universal precautions when appropriate.
CALL 9-1-1 or the local emergency number for the following situations:
➤ The athlete is unconscious, confused, or seems to be losing consciousness.
➤ The athlete has breathing difficulty or is breathing irregularly.
➤ The athlete has persistent chest pain or pressure.
➤ The athlete has pressure or pain in the abdomen that does not go away.
➤ The athlete is vomiting or passing blood.
➤ The athlete has a seizure, severe headache, or slurred speech.
➤ The athlete appears to have been poisoned.
➤ The athlete has injuries to the head, neck, or back.
➤ You are unsure how to handle the problem.
➤ You are unsure about the severity of the illness.
CARE:
1. Check for the signals of an allergic reaction, such as breathing difficulty, a feeling of tightness in the chest and throat, and swelling of the face, neck, and tongue.
2. Care for any life-threatening conditions first.
3. Help the athlete rest comfortably.
4. To minimize shock, keep the athlete from getting chilled or overheated.
5. Reassure the athlete.

6. Watch for changes in consciousness, breathing, and pulse.
7. *Do not give anything to eat or drink unless the athlete is fully conscious.*
8. Care for any problems that develop, such as vomiting (p. 167), unconsciousness (p. 166), or stopped breathing (p. 91).

See also Sudden illness—Diabetic emergency (below), Sudden illness—Seizure (p. 160), and Sudden illness— Stroke (p. 161).

Sudden Illness—Diabetic Emergency

Diabetes is a condition in which the body is unable to balance insulin and sugar levels in the body. You will not be able to tell what the body needs. Giving sugar will not cause additional harm.

You may know that the athlete is diabetic, or you may see a medical alert bracelet. If there is no evidence that the athlete is diabetic, then give care as for sudden illness (p. 157).

SIGNALS OF DIABETIC EMERGENCY
➤ Medical alert bracelet
➤ Feeling lightheaded, dizzy, confused, or weak
➤ Irregular breathing
➤ Irregular pulse
➤ Feeling or looking ill
➤ May become unconscious

First Aid Steps
CHECK the scene for safety. **CHECK** the injured athlete, following universal precautions when appropriate.
CALL 9-1-1 or the local emergency number if there are any signals of a serious condition.

CARE:
1. If the athlete is conscious and a known diabetic, give sugar (fruit juices, candy, nondiet drinks, table sugar).
2. If the athlete is not feeling better in about 5 minutes, send someone to call EMS personnel.

▶ *If the athlete becomes unconscious—*
3. Send someone to call 9-1-1 or the local emergency number if you have not done so already.
4. Check breathing and pulse and care for the conditions you find.

See Breathing—Stopped (p. 91) and CPR (p. 110).
5. *Do not give anything to eat or drink.*
See also Sudden illness (p. 157).

▼ SUDDEN ILLNESS—SEIZURE

A seizure is a loss of body control that occurs when brain functions are disrupted by injury or illness. Seizure disorders include epilepsy and can usually be controlled by medication, although the athlete may still have occasional seizures. The goals for care are to protect the athlete from injury during the seizure, ensure that the airway stays open, and call EMS personnel when appropriate.

SIGNALS OF SEIZURE

➤ Mild seizure may be a short, temporary blackout.
➤ Major seizure may be sudden, uncontrolled muscular contractions (convulsions) of part of or the entire body.
➤ The athlete may have an unusual sensation (aura) before the seizure occurs.
➤ Presence of Medical Alert bracelet for seizure disorder.

FIRST AID STEPS

CHECK the scene for safety. **CHECK** the injured athlete, following universal precautions when appropriate.

CALL 9-1-1 or the local emergency number UNLESS you know the athlete has a seizure disorder or epilepsy. Even if the athlete has epilepsy, call EMS personnel if—

➤ The seizure lasts longer than a few minutes or is repeated.
➤ The athlete does not regain consciousness.
➤ The athlete is pregnant, known to be a diabetic, or is injured.

CARE:

1. Remove nearby objects that might cause injury.
2. Protect the athlete's head by placing a folded towel or clothing beneath it.
3. *Do not hold or restrain the athlete.*
4. *Do not place anything between the athlete's teeth.*
5. Place the athlete on the side to drain fluids from his or her mouth.
6. When the seizure is over, check for breathing and other injuries. If necessary, perform rescue breathing (see Breathing—Stopped, p. 91) or CPR (p. 110).
7. Reassure and comfort the athlete.
8. Stay with the athlete until he or she is fully conscious, oriented to the surroundings, and able to care for himself or herself.

See also Sudden illness (p. 157).

▼ SUDDEN ILLNESS—STROKE

A stroke is a disruption of blood flow to a part of the brain serious enough to damage brain tissue, often resulting when a blood vessel bursts or becomes narrowed by a clot. Stroke may also result from a head injury, high blood pressure, or other conditions. The goals of care are to get emergency medical help quickly and prevent further problems while waiting for EMS personnel to arrive.

SIGNALS OF STROKE
➤ Looking or feeling ill
➤ Sudden weakness and numbness of the face, arm, or leg, usually on one side
➤ Difficulty talking
➤ Difficulty understanding speech
➤ Blurred or dimmed vision
➤ Unequal pupil size
➤ Sudden severe headache
➤ Dizziness, confusion
➤ Ringing in the ears
➤ Loss of bladder or bowel control
➤ Loss of consciousness

FIRST AID STEPS
CHECK the scene for safety. **CHECK** the injured athlete, following universal precautions when appropriate. **CALL** 9-1-1 or the local emergency number. **CARE:**
1. Care for the specific conditions you find. Keep the airway open if the athlete becomes unconscious.
2. If the athlete is drooling or having difficulty swallowing, place on his or her side to keep the airway clear.
3. Try to reassure the athlete.
4. Help the athlete rest in a comfortable position.
5. *Do not give the athlete anything to eat or drink.*
See also Sudden illness (p. 157).

▼ SUNBURN

Sunburn usually is a superficial burn and does not require emergency care. Prevention is important to avoid long-term effects of too much sun, such as skin cancer.

First Aid Steps

CHECK the scene for safety. **CHECK** the injured athlete, following universal precautions when appropriate.

CALL 9-1-1 or the local emergency number if there are signals of a serious condition.

CARE:

1. Cool the burn.
2. Wash the area with soap and water and keep the area clean.
3. Prevent further damage by staying out of the sun or wearing a protective lotion.
4. Your doctor or pharmacist may recommend products for sunburn care.

▶ *If the skin blisters—*

5. Protect unbroken blisters with loose bandages.
6. Keep broken blisters clean to prevent infection. Apply an antibiotic cream and watch for signals of infection.

See also Burns (p. 95).

▼ Sweating—Unusual

Sweating without an appropriate obvious cause (exertion or exercise) may be a signal of a serious condition. Check for other signals. If the athlete is sweating unusually heavily or if the athlete has other signals, consider the conditions listed here and give care for the appropriate problem. Otherwise, provide the care for sudden illness (p. 157).

➤ Breathing difficulty (p. 89)
➤ Chest pain or pressure (p. 102)
➤ Heat-related emergencies (p. 139)
➤ Internal injury (p. 131)
➤ Poisoning (p. 145)
➤ Shock (p. 150)
➤ Substance abuse (p. 156)

SWELLING

Swelling is a common signal of musculoskeletal injuries. See Bone and joint injuries (p. 88) and Muscle Injury (p. 137).

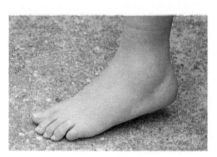

Swelling of a body area may also result from abdominal injury (p. 64), the bite or sting of an insect or animal (pp. 74–85), a burn (p. 95), exposure to a poisonous plant (p. 144), such as poison ivy, and internal injury (p. 131).

Swelling of the face and mouth, and in particular the tissues of the airway, typically signals an allergic reaction (p. 66). In any instance of an allergic reaction, call 9-1-1 or the local emergency number immediately.

TEETH—KNOCKED OUT

Teeth may be knocked out in any injury involving the mouth or head. The goals of care are to check for any additional serious injury, care for the bleeding inside the mouth, and preserve the tooth for possible reimplantation.

FIRST AID STEPS

CHECK the scene for safety. **CHECK** the injured athlete, following universal precautions.

CALL 9-1-1 or the local emergency number if there are signals of a serious condition.

CARE:

1. Have the athlete bite down on a rolled sterile dressing in the space left by the tooth.

2. Save any displaced teeth:
   • Pick up teeth by the crown (white part), not the root.
   • Place them in milk, if possible, or water.
3. Call a dentist immediately for instructions on further care.

If the athlete's teeth were knocked out by significant impact, also evaluate the athlete for a head injury (p. 123) and back or neck injury (p. 68).

See also Mouth injury (p. 133), Wounds (p. 171), and Head injury (p. 123).

▼ TICK BITE *(see Bites and stings—Tick bite, p. 83)*

▼ TRANSPORTING AN INJURED ATHLETE

Some musculoskeletal injuries are obviously minor and do not require professional medical care. Others are obviously more serious and may require you to call EMS personnel. If you discover a life-threatening emergency or think it likely for one to develop, send someone to call EMS personnel and wait for help. Always call EMS personnel for any injury involving the following:

➤ Severe bleeding
➤ Injuries to the head, neck, or back
➤ Possible broken bones that may be difficult to transport properly, such as the hip and legs

Fractures of large bones may bleed internally or externally and are likely to cause shock (p. 150). *Do not attempt to transport an athlete with such an injury.*

Some injuries are not serious enough for you to call EMS personnel but may still require professional medical care. If you decide to transport the injured athlete yourself to a medical facility, follow the general rule: *When in doubt, splint.*

Always splint the injury before moving the athlete. If possible, have someone drive you so you can continue to provide care.

See also Moving an injured athlete (p. 134).

UNCONSCIOUSNESS

Unconsciousness, a state in which the athlete is completely unresponsive to touch and any sensory stimulus, is both a life-threatening emergency in itself and possibly a signal of a serious condition needing immediate care. Unconsciousness results from the brain not receiving enough oxygen, but this may be caused by a long list of injuries and illnesses. The goals of care are to get the athlete immediate medical help and care for whatever condition you find.

The athlete may not be unconscious when first found. **Consciousness that diminishes and then becomes unconsciousness usually signals a serious decline in the athlete's condition and requires immediate emergency help.**

First Aid Steps

CHECK the scene for safety. **CHECK** the athlete, following universal precautions when appropriate, for signals of possible causes of the unconsciousness:

➤ Back or neck injury (p. 68)
➤ Chest pain or pressure (p. 102)
➤ Choking (p. 104)
➤ Cold-related emergencies (p. 108)
➤ Concussion (see Head injury, p. 123)
➤ Electrical burn (p. 118)
➤ Fainting (p. 121)
➤ Head injury (p. 123)
➤ Heat-related emergencies (p. 139)
➤ Internal injury (p. 131)
➤ Poisoning (p. 145)
➤ Shock (p. 150)
➤ Smoke inhalation (p. 151)
➤ Substance abuse (p. 156)
➤ Sudden illness (p. 157)
➤ Sudden illness—Diabetic emergency (p. 159)
➤ Sudden illness—Seizure (p. 160)
➤ Sudden illness—Stroke (p. 161)

CALL 9-1-1 or the local emergency number even if the athlete regains consciousness because the athlete may still have a life-threatening condition.

CARE:

1. Check breathing. Position the athlete on the side to keep the airway open and allow fluids to drain from the mouth.

▼Vomiting

Vomiting without an obvious cause may be a signal of a serious condition. Check for other signals. If the athlete's vomiting is without explanation or is especially severe or if the athlete has other signals, consider the problems listed here and give the appropriate care:

➤ Head injury (p. 123) or Back or neck injury (p. 68)
➤ Heat-related emergencies (p. 139)
➤ Internal injury (p. 131)
➤ Poisoning (p. 145)
➤ Sudden illness (p. 157)

First Aid Steps

CHECK the scene for safety. **CHECK** the injured athlete, following universal precautions when appropriate.
CALL 9-1-1 or the local emergency number for any athlete who vomits blood or an athlete with possible heat stroke who vomits.
CARE:
1. Keep the airway open.
2. Turn an unconscious athlete on the side to let the mouth drain.
3. Wipe the mouth clean.
4. Give additional care as needed.

▼ Wasp Sting *(see Bites and stings—Bee sting, p. 75)*

▌Water Rescue

Emergencies can happen to anyone in, on, or around the water, regardless of how good a swimmer the athlete is or the nature of the activity. Being able to recognize an athlete who is having trouble in the water may help save the athlete's life. Since the athlete may not be able to call for help, it is important to know the signals of an emergency.

SIGNALS OF NEAR-DROWNING

➤ Struggling movements; little or no forward progress.
➤ The athlete may or may not be able to call or signal for help.
➤ The athlete struggles to breathe.

FIRST AID STEPS

CHECK the scene for safety.
CALL 9-1-1 or the local emergency number.
CARE:

1. Attempt to rescue by reaching or throwing a floating object to the athlete (see Water rescue methods, below).
2. *Do not attempt a swimming rescue unless trained to do so.*

▶ *Once the athlete is out of the water—*
Follow universal precautions.

3. Check the athlete.
4. Care for any conditions you find. See Breathing— Stopped (p. 91) and CPR (p. 110).

See also Drowning (p. 115).

WATER RESCUE METHODS

The safest methods are reaching, throwing, and wading assists. In most cases, at least one of these methods will be successful.

Reaching assist

Reaching assist

Throwing assist

Wading assist

WHEEZING *(see Breathing difficulty, p. 89 and Choking, p. 104)*

Wounds

A wound is an injury to the skin and underlying soft tissues. Damage to blood vessels causes bleeding. When caring for wounds, the goals of care are to control bleeding, prevent infection, and minimize shock.

SIGNALS OF WOUNDS

➤ Cuts, scrapes, punctures, or other breaks in the skin
➤ Bleeding
➤ Bruising
➤ Swelling

FIRST AID STEPS

CHECK the scene for safety. **CHECK** the injured athlete, following universal precautions when appropriate.

CALL 9-1-1 or the local emergency number for the following situations:

➤ Bleeding that cannot be stopped
➤ Wounds that show muscle or bone, involve joints, gape widely, or involve hands or feet
➤ Large or deep wounds
➤ Large or deeply embedded objects in the wound *(Do not remove embedded objects.)*
➤ Human or animal bites
➤ Any wound that would leave an obvious scar, such as on the face
➤ Skin or body parts that have been partially or completely torn away

CARE:

1. Cover the wound with a sterile gauze pad and press firmly against the wound. (Use your bare hand to apply pressure only as a last resort.)
2. If bleeding continues, use pressure, elevation, and bandaging to control the bleeding. Add more dressings as needed. For complete care, see Bleeding, p. 85.

3. In cases of serious bleeding, shock is likely; give care to minimize shock (p. 150).
4. If the wound was caused by an object that could carry infection, check with a doctor whether a tetanus booster may be needed.

See also Bleeding (p. 85), Wounds—Abrasion (below), Wounds—Amputation (p. 173), Wounds—Embedded object (p. 173), and Wounds—Puncture (p. 175).

WOUNDS—ABRASION

An abrasion is a type of wound in which the skin has been rubbed or scraped away. An important goal of care is to prevent infection, as dirt or other foreign matter is often ground into the wound.

SIGNALS OF ABRASION
➤ Raw, red area
➤ Minimal bleeding (may be oozing)
➤ Pain

FIRST AID STEPS
CHECK the scene for safety. **CHECK** the injured athlete, following universal precautions when appropriate.
CALL 9-1-1 or the local emergency number if there are signals of any serious condition.
CARE:
1. Wash the wound with soap and warm water.
2. Place a sterile dressing over the wound.
3. Apply direct pressure for a few minutes if needed to control bleeding.
4. When bleeding is controlled, remove the dressing and apply an antibiotic ointment.
5. Apply a new dressing and bandage.

▶ *If the abrasion was caused by an object that may carry infection—*

6. Check with a doctor whether a tetanus booster may be necessary.

▶ *If bleeding does not stop immediately—*

7. Give additional care to stop bleeding: elevate the limb and maintain pressure with a bandage. See Bleeding, p. 85.

For more serious wounds, see Wounds (p. 171).

▼Wounds—Amputation

Amputation is a wound in which a part of the body has been torn or cut off. The goals of first aid are to care for the wound and maintain the severed body part for potential surgical reattachment.

First Aid Steps

CHECK the scene for safety. **CHECK** the injured athlete, following universal precautions when appropriate.
CALL 9-1-1 or the local emergency number.
CARE:

1. Control bleeding (p. 85).
2. Wrap and bandage the wound to prevent infection.
3. If bleeding is significant, give care to minimize shock (p. 150).
4. Wrap the severed body part in sterile gauze or a clean cloth.
5. Place the severed part in a plastic bag.
6. Put the plastic bag on ice (but do not freeze it) and keep it with the athlete.

See also Wounds (p. 171).

▼Wounds—Embedded Object

An embedded object is any object still in an athlete's wound, whether it is a piece of glass, a knife, or any other object. The object in the wound may be putting pressure on blood vessels that otherwise could cause serious bleeding and therefore should not be removed from the wound. The goals of care are to control bleeding, prevent infection, and minimize shock.

First Aid Steps

CHECK the scene for safety. **CHECK** the injured athlete, following universal precautions when appropriate. **CALL** 9-1-1 or the local emergency number.
CARE:
1. *Do not remove the object.*
2. Bandage bulky dressings around the object to support the object in place.

3. Bandage the dressing in place.

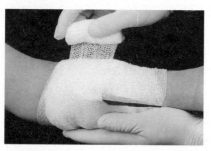

4. Because shock is likely if bleeding is severe, give care to minimize shock (p. 150).

See also Wounds (p. 171).

For an object in the eye, see also Eye injury (p. 119).

WOUNDS—PUNCTURE

Puncture wounds may be serious because internal tissues may be damaged and because often microorganisms are trapped inside the wound, making infection more likely. Severe bleeding is rare in puncture wounds unless a major blood vessel is injured. The goals of care are to control bleeding and prevent infection.

SIGNALS OF PUNCTURE WOUND

➤ Red hole in skin
➤ Redness in area of puncture
➤ Possible object embedded in wound

FIRST AID STEPS

CHECK the scene for safety. **CHECK** the injured athlete, following universal precautions when appropriate.

CALL 9-1-1 or the local emergency number for—
➤ Bleeding that cannot be stopped.
➤ Wounds that show muscle or bone, involve joints, gape widely, or involve the hands or feet.
➤ Large or deep wounds.
➤ Large or deeply embedded objects in the wound. (*Do not remove embedded objects.*)
➤ Human or animal bites.
➤ Any wound that would leave an obvious scar, such as on the face.
➤ Skin or body parts that have been partially or completely torn away.

CARE:
1. Except for a small object like a splinter, do not remove an embedded object from the wound. Bandage around the object (see Wounds—Embedded object, p. 173).
2. Send someone to call EMS personnel for a serious wound (see following).
3. Cover the wound with a sterile gauze pad and press firmly against the wound. (Use your bare hand to apply pressure only as a last resort.)
4. In cases of serious bleeding, shock is likely; give care to minimize shock (p. 150).

▶ *If bleeding continues—*
5. Use pressure, elevation, and bandaging to control the bleeding. Add more dressings as needed. For complete care steps, see Bleeding, p. 85.

▶ *If the puncture wound was caused by an object that could carry infection—*
6. Check with a doctor whether a tetanus booster may be needed.

See also Wounds (p. 171).